Praise for *Raising Kids for True Greatness*

"*Raising Kids for True Greatness* is an important message for our times. It is clear, compelling, and full of common sense. It's not only loaded with practical, usable information, but is a guide you will read and reread. Both your mind and your heart will tell you this book is true."

—Dr. Gary Smalley
Author, *The DNA of Relationships*

"How much energy do we spend trying to raise our children to be great in the eyes of the world rather than in the eyes of our God? Dr. Kimmel's book cuts to the core of what parents need to understand in order to raise kids for true greatness."

—Pastor Jim Cymbala, The Brooklyn Tabernacle

"All parents want their children to be successful, but many have a very vague idea of what that means. Dr. Tim Kimmel clears the air and helps parents not only identify true success, but gives helpful guidelines on how to raise children who will accomplish their potential for God in the world."

—Gary D. Chapman, PhD
Author, *The Five Love Languages* and *The Four Seasons of Marriage*

"What does true greatness look like for a Christian? Author Tim Kimmel helps us weed out the common worldly view of greatness and teaches us to plant seeds of lasting value into the lives of our children. *Raising Kids for True Greatness* leads each of us as parents down the right road of making a positive and significant impact on the next generation."

—Karol Ladd
Author, *The Power of a Positive Mom* and
A Positive Plan for Creating More Calm, Less Stress

"The wise parent will use Tim Kimmel's exceptional book, first, to learn what true greatness is. Learning to understand true greatness will take some effort and may require some change in perspective on genuine life values—but it will lead you to maturity. Once the parent grasps the meaning of true greatness they will find guidance in passing these priceless virtues on to their child. In this new, negative culture in which we find ourselves, we parents must know and understand the principles of this book. Only then will we enable our children to not only succeed, but to lead godly lives."

—Ross Campbell, MD
Associate Professor of Pediatrics and Child Psychiatry, University of Tennessee
Author, *How to Really Love Your Child* and *How to Really Parent Your Child*

RAISING KIDS
FOR **TRUE**
GREATNESS

redefine success for you and your child

DR. TIM KIMMEL

W Publishing Group
A Division of Thomas Nelson Publishers
Since 1798

www.wpublishinggroup.com

RAISING KIDS FOR TRUE GREATNESS

© 2006 Tim Kimmel

Published by W Publishing Group, a division of Thomas Nelson, Inc., P.O. Box
141000, Nashville, TN 37214.

All Scripture quotations, unless otherwise indicated, are taken from The Holy Bible,
New International Version. Copyright © 1973, 1978, 1984 by International Bible
Society. Used by permission of Zondervan. All rights reserved. Other Scripture quota-
tions are taken from the following: New King James Version® (NKJV®). Copyright ©
1982 by Thomas Nelson, Inc. Used by permission. All rights reserved. The New
Century Version® (NCV®). Copyright © 1987, 1988, 1991 by Thomas Nelson, Inc.
Used by permission. All rights reserved.

Cover Design: gearbox
Interior Design: Stacy Clark

Library of Congress Cataloging-in-Publication Data

Kimmel, Tim.
Raising kids for true greatness : redefine success for you and your child / Tim
Kimmel.
       p. cm.
Includes bibliographical references.
      ISBN-10: 0-8499-0951-1
      ISBN-13: 978-0-8499-0951-1
      1. Parenting—Religious aspects—Christianity. 2. Child rearing—
Religious aspects—Christianity. I. Title.
      BV4529.K552 2006
      248.8'45—dc22

                                                                  2005034990

Printed in the United States of America

06 07 08 09 10 RRD 9 8 7 6 5 4

CONTENTS

To Steve and Barbara Uhlmann

If you want to see what true greatness looks
like, just follow these two people around.

ACKNOWLEDGMENTS

This was not an easy book to capture. The fact is that if you're writing about something as important and extraordinary as true greatness, it shouldn't be easy. But there were some key people who slipped in through the seams of my life at the right time to help me move this message from the abstract to the concrete, from the complex to the simple. I'm in debt to people like . . .

. . . Steve and Cheryl Green, the A-team of author development, fellow pilgrims, and loyal friends.

. . . the staff of W Publishing Group, with standouts like David Moberg and Debbie Wickwire. From conception to delivery, you are the kind of people an author wants surrounding him as he turns big ideas into something that everyone can make their own.

. . . editor Jennifer Stair. I've never known anyone who can nip and tuck words as well as you.

. . . the staff and board of directors of Family Matters®. It's easy to focus on the challenge before me when such capable people have my back.

. . . and Steve and Barbara Uhlmann. Without the keys to

your hideaway in the mountains, this book would still be float-ing around in my head.

What made this message on true greatness make the most sense to me are the people who surround me each day and model what greatness looks like lived out at street level. Like Darcy. You put the *soul* in "soul mate," and you are the heart behind this message. Mike, Karis, Cody, Shiloh, and Colt: you've made it fun to prove that true greatness actually works before I captured it in words. And two fabulous granddaugh-ters, Riley and Lydia . . . you're next.

INTRODUCTION

WHY SUCCESS ISN'T ENOUGH

He was the most spectacular sprinter in America. Dubbed "the fastest man alive," Bobby Hayes became a global celebrity at the 1964 Tokyo Olympics, winning the gold medal for the 100 meters and running the 400-relay anchor leg in an astonishing 8.6 seconds. Nobody before or since has run that fast. As one sportswriter put it, "It's barely human to run that fast. . . . That's a *blur*."[1]

The next year, Hayes took his world-class speed to the Dallas Cowboys, gained more than 1,000 yards that season, and led the NFL in yards per catch as well as touchdowns scored. He was so fast that opposing teams had to play a zone defense against him, because no one man could cover him when he went out for a pass.[2]

Throughout the early 1970s, Bobby "The Bullet" Hayes ruled the world of football. And to this day, he is still the only athlete to have both an Olympic gold medal and a Super Bowl ring. At the height of his game, Hayes was getting positive ink in the sports sections of newspapers all over the country. His action shots were part of the backdrop in many sports bars, and his poster adorned thousands of kids' bedroom walls.

Everyone, it seemed, knew the name of "the fastest man

alive." And fathers all across America encouraged their sons that if they worked hard enough, they, too, could grow up to be like the great Bobby Hayes.

Aiming Higher

What is your goal when it comes to raising your children? If you're like most parents, the word *success* is somewhere in your answer. We all want the very best for our children. We want them to get a good education, have prestigious jobs, live in safe neighborhoods, marry spouses who are easy to look at, and someday have wonderful children of their own. And who is kidding whom? Deep down, we wouldn't mind it a bit if our children someday became as legendary and successful in their chosen professions as Bobby Hayes became in his, right?

To be fair, there is a sense of success that is a legitimate parenting goal, if we're defining *success* as our children doing something productive with their talents and skills that enables them to be independent, happy adults.

The problem is that most parents don't stop there. They add the wealth, power, beauty, and fame I mentioned above to their definition. The telltale sign that these goals have a vise grip on their view of success is the heavy emphasis they place on their kids' getting stellar grades, being connected to the influential kids in school, getting onto winning teams, racking up strong athletic statistics, being the chosen leaders of their various endeavors, and investing often and heavily in current fashion. These are the priorities that plant the seeds of success—the wealth, power, beauty, and fame kind—into the soil of their kids' souls. If their children are successful—in these ways that our society defines *success*—then these parents sit back, relax, and congratulate themselves on a job well done.

But is that enough? Is that all we want our children to be—merely *successful*?

It may surprise you to learn that we don't really need God's help to raise successful kids, especially ones aimed at these standard goals of success. Our unchurched friends and neighbors are raising their children to reach those same goals, and most of them do an exceptional job of preparing their kids for a successful life. I have little doubt that most of their children will grow up to achieve their parents' dreams for them.

> A person can be *successful* without coming close to being truly *great*. And wouldn't we all rather aim our children toward true greatness?

But a person can be *successful* without coming close to being truly *great*. And wouldn't we all rather aim our children toward true greatness?

I'm not saying that there's anything inherently wrong with getting a good education, making a nice living, and being well known. These things are fine additions to an adult life—but they shouldn't be the primary goals we set for our children. That's because man-made success has little to do with true greatness.

Here's what I'm suggesting in this book: if we're aiming our children at success, we're aiming far too low. We're going to invest twenty years of our lives and spend tons of money preparing our kids for the future. Why not prepare them for a life that dwarfs the goals of those who are merely successful? Why not groom our children for true greatness?

○ Success looks inward; true greatness looks upward, then outward.

○ Success is about my agenda; true greatness is about God's agenda.

○ Success accommodates selfishness; true greatness celebrates altruism.

○ Success is about receiving; true greatness is about giving.

○ Success worships what it sees in a mirror; true greatness grieves over what it sees through its windows.

○ Success pays off for now; true greatness pays off forever.

Raising Kids Right

As we will see throughout this book, *true greatness is a passionate love for God that demonstrates itself in an unquenchable love and concern for others.*

It reminds me of a man named Nick and his wife, Drana. She was a homemaker, and Nick was a competent businessman. They had a good-sized house in the decent neighborhood and enough money to make most of their dreams come true. To the casual observer, it was evident that Nick and Drana were going to see their children follow in their footsteps and achieve many of the benefits that a successful adult life has to offer.

But Nick and Drana weren't content with such trivial goals; they wanted a far more significant life for their kids. They wanted to raise kids who gave back to life much more than they took.

And as parents, they knew that their example carried more clout with their children than their words ever could. That's why their home was often a stopover for strangers or people who needed a place to regroup. They used their resources to lighten the burden that many unfortunate people around them had to carry.

> True greatness is a passionate love for God that demonstrates itself in an unquenchable love and concern for others.

On top of that, they didn't see church as a place to merely park and watch on Sunday but as a launching point for an attitude of service seven days a week. They sang in the choir and volunteered in church ministries that enabled them to put sweat on their faith.

Their youngest daughter, Agnes, developed an unquenchable longing to use her life to do something that would outlive her. She passionately desired to turn her love for God into actions that affected people for His glory and for their personal good.

Agnes was smart, attractive, and industrious, but these attributes meant little to her. She learned from her parents that the best things you have to offer in life come from your heart, not your head; from your character, not your charm; from your love, not your looks. Her heart spilled over with authentic kindness, and she was willing to put herself at great risk to share that kindness with the people who needed it most.

As a young woman, Agnes decided to devote her life to showing grace and mercy to "the poorest of the poor"—the people nobody else was willing to reach out to. She ministered among the most dangerous criminals and in the worst conditions known to humankind. She loved God and she loved others. Everything about her personal and professional life brought glory to God by bringing hope to as many people as she could.

During her career, she started a movement called the "Sisters of Charity." She also borrowed the name of an unassuming Catholic nun who believed in the "little way"—working for good by carrying out very simple tasks joyfully. Agnes ended up unintentionally branding this name into everyone's mind as someone who has lived a life of true greatness. The world knew Agnes as Mother Teresa.

Without setting out to do anything more than love the hard to love, this lady personally touched hundreds of thousands of lives, raised millions of dollars to help the poor, and was awarded the Nobel Peace Prize for her efforts.

Nick and Drana didn't aim their daughter at money or fame; they simply raised her to make a difference in the world. And the success their daughter experienced was not driven by her résumé or by some strategic plan; rather, it was the kind of success that often accompanies people who want to use their lives to do something that makes people better off and God better served.

The road that Mother Teresa took was long, lonely, and often crowded with inexhaustible needs, but it led her to a life of true greatness.

Why Not Raise Your Kids for True Greatness?

"Oh, come on," I can hear some of you protesting. "You've got to be kidding me! You're leading off your argument by using Mother Teresa as an illustration of what true greatness looks like? Earth to Tim: my child is never going to be a Mother Teresa."

Before you shut this book and head back to the store for a refund, let me ask you one question:

Why not?

While I'm at it, let me ask you a few more. Why do we dream such small dreams and expect so little from our children? Why do we assume that we have such limited capabilities as parents? Why do we assume that great people have to be the exception rather than the rule when it comes to our efforts as parents? Why don't we think that our children can ever take rank among the truly great? Worse, why do we sell God's bigger plan for our lives short?

Obviously, there are no guarantees in life. And I'm not in any way suggesting that if you read this book and apply what you learn, your child will become the next Mother Teresa.

But, then again, she might. Your sons and daughters have the potential of making an extraordinary difference in life. And they don't have to join the Sisters of Charity or live the life of a monk to pull it off! Most kids would love the chance to live their lives for something more than merely what is in it for them. Wouldn't you like to find out how?

If so, this book is for you. Read on.

chapter one

THE LONG AND WINDING ROAD TO GREATNESS

M any parents are so busy preparing their children for success that they miss the chance to equip them to do something truly extraordinary. Somewhere along the way, they've taken a wrong turn in their thinking and are pointing their children toward misdirected goals.

According to most parents, a child's success starts with a good education. So they become preoccupied with their child's grades, class placement, cumulative GPA, and SAT scores. They make this a high priority—for many, the highest—because they think that a good education is the best way for their children to obtain a prestigious career—another way of saying, a job that pays well.

Why do parents want their children to make a lot of money? So they can live in attractive homes in a safe part of town and have an enviable lifestyle. And while they're at it, maybe their respectable jobs will help them find spouses who look good in the Christmas pictures, and then they can bring home lots of cute grandchildren for Grandma and Grandpa to enjoy.

If all goes according to plan, these parents reason, their children will achieve the kind of success that enables them to enjoy an adult life of comfort and endless personal opportunities.

Well paid, well supplied, well known, and well received—these are the standard characteristics of a successful life.

> According to Jesus, if we want our kids to be truly great, we must first teach them to be servants.

Parents whose children achieve these goals often experience an overwhelming sense of relief: "I did it. I handed my kids a powerful gift. I helped them achieve success."

God Has Bigger and Better Plans for Our Kids

Question: where in the Bible does it say that we are supposed to aim our kids at these priorities for success? If anything, these run counter to what the Bible encourages us to pursue. Wealth, fame, and comfort can be nice additions that our children might gain by default on their way to a great life. But we find ourselves on biblical thin ice if we make them the targets at which we are aiming our kids.

Jesus weighed in on this subject, and His observation might surprise you. Here's what He had to say about what it means to be truly great:

You know that the rulers of the non-Jewish people love to show their power over the people. And their important leaders love to use all their authority. But it should not be that way among you. *Whoever wants to become great among you must serve the rest of you like a servant.* Whoever wants to become first among you must serve the rest of you like a slave. In the same way, the Son of Man did not come to be served. He came to serve others and to give his life as a ransom for many people. (Matthew 20:25–28 NCV, emphasis added)

According to Jesus, if we want our kids to be truly great, we must first teach them to be servants. But let's face it: most parents aren't raising their children to serve others; they're raising their kids to be served by others. Their success mantra rings hollow: "Be first! Own the best! Be the boss! Don't let anyone get in your way! It's all compare, compete, and control!"

But this materialistic view of success finds no home in the heart of God. God has much bigger and better plans for our children than merely indulging them. He has called our children to a much higher set of goals than what this world has to offer.

God's goals for our children often run counter to the default mode of the human heart—especially a heart that has built its hope on the Carpenter from Galilee. That's why God has put parents into the equation. We offer the best means to help our children make true greatness the ultimate goal of their lives.

> God has much bigger and better plans for our children than merely indulging them.

Parenting on Purpose

I can think of three compelling reasons to avoid the trap of aiming your kids toward a life of success.

First, they never get to have the significant impact that God intended for them. God has gifted them and wants to use their experiences and relationships to do something that is beyond quantification. They may still have prestigious careers, but they'll carry out their work for a much better reason than what's in it for them.

Second, the pursuit of man-made success often brings out the worst in both parents and children. Many kids who are aimed at success struggle with antagonism or indifference toward their parents' dreams for them.

The third reason you want to avoid the success trap is that you really undermine the chance for your kids to gain the kind of wealth and extravagance God intended for them to enjoy . . . in heaven.

God would like to build your children a mansion that is the logical extension of their faithfulness here on earth. If you've visited the Rocky Mountains or gazed over the edge of the Grand Canyon, you know that God is a superb architect. And if you've peeked at a sunset lately, you realize that God has a good eye for color. It makes so much more sense to raise your kids to live faithful and effective lives on earth and then leave the breadth of their success up to God. Eventually, He can create a far more "successful" future—even a forever future—than the best-laid human plans ever could.

The Trinity of True Greatness

True greatness takes on a life of its own when it is applied to the three biggest challenges our children must face. For the record, there are three primary questions your children need to answer in order to enjoy an effective adult life. If they answer these three questions correctly, they will be able to leave a powerful and lasting legacy for many generations to come:

1. What is my mission in life going to be?
2. Who is my mate going to be?
3. Who is my master going to be?

Put another way: What am I going to do with my life? Who will I spend my life with? Who will I live it for?

Here's what makes aiming your children at true greatness so compelling: their ability to answer these three questions properly almost becomes a foregone conclusion. When you're consistently pointing your kids toward greatness, it's difficult for them to mess up these three profound dimensions of their lives.

As we have said, true greatness happens when we produce kids who have

> We simply have to show our kids what true greatness looks like with our lives.

a passionate love for God that shows itself in an unquenchable love and concern for others. This greatness is maximized when our children thoroughly prepare to make the best contribution possible through their gifts and skills, team their dreams with someone who multiplies their capabilities, and do everything in complete submission to the God who called them to true greatness in the first place.

And oftentimes, we can embed the priorities of true greatness into the DNA of our children's character without having to formally teach them how to do it. We simply have to show our kids what true greatness looks like with our lives.

WHERE ARE YOU AIMING YOUR KIDS?

1. Look at your calendar. How much of your time do you spend nurturing an "others-oriented" attitude in your children?
2. Look at your checkbook. How much of your resources are going to serving others rather than yourselves?
3. Look at your attitude. What makes you feel like you are doing a good job at raising your kids?
4. Look at your heart. What are the things that bring joy and satisfaction to you and to your family?
5. Look at your reputation. How would your friends, coworkers, teachers, and neighbors characterize your priorities?

You see, as parents, we play the greatest role in how our children answer these questions. Either we put them on the freeway to success, or we point them toward the long and winding road that leads to true greatness.

There aren't many parents willing to take on this challenge. It's too bad, because raising kids for greatness has more immediate as well as long-term benefits for Mom and Dad than raising them merely for successfulness. Among other things, greatness goals improve the way your children view you, treat you, and blend into the dynamic of your family.

Because the freeway to success is easier to quantify and requires far less from the parents from a faith perspective, many parents prefer to take the shortcut. And let's face it: success does offer some nice amenities for your kids, if you're willing to confine their rewards to the narrow options of what earth has to offer. But it's best to keep in perspective that the greatest rewards that earth has to offer pale in comparison to the minimum that a life of true greatness has to give.

On top of that, it's hard to send kids down a path you aren't willing to take yourself. In most cases, this is the main reason parents are satisfied with the mediocrity of success when it comes to their children's future. However, we should keep in mind that regardless of how rugged the path to greatness may look, our kids would rather we show them the way than merely point them in the general direction.

> The greatest rewards that earth has to offer pale in comparison to the minimum that a life of true greatness has to give.

Should you choose to be their tour guide on the long and winding road to true greatness, you'll find that you have more help than you ever imagined along the way. The Author and Sustainer of true greatness will be with you. He'll be glad to whisper in your ear and place His nail-scarred hand on your shoulder anytime you need a nudge in the right direction.

True greatness is the only legitimate choice when it comes to preparing your kids for their adult lives. As C. S. Lewis wisely pointed out, "Aim at heaven, and you will get earth thrown in. Aim at earth, and you get neither." God wants to give your children a life that can't be measured by space or confined by time.

In the pages that follow, I will show you how you can prepare your children for a life of extraordinary greatness.

And guess what? If you give your kids the gift of true greatness, God will often throw in earthly *success* . . . for free.

Ten Ways to Be a Great Member of the Family

1. Everybody helps everybody . . . always, in whatever ways are needed.
2. Be upbeat, positive, and encouraging.
3. Remember, "please" and "thank you" are not just good manners; they're the calling cards of a grateful heart.
4. Have a lot of fun, just not at the expense of anyone else.
5. Each week, do your best to eat as many meals as possible together as a family. You'll cut the chance of your kids using tobacco and drugs in half and double the chances they'll bring home A's on their report cards![3]
6. Respect one another's space and stuff. Ask, and it most likely will be given unto you.
7. Guard family traditions, and do your best to celebrate all birthdays, holidays, and major milestones.
8. Guard the morals and integrity of everyone around you. Be sensitive about how you communicate, what you view, and whom you bring into the family circle.
9. Be quick to rally around a family member who is down, whether it's a result of sickness, injury, failure, rejection, or discouragement.

10. Assume that the Lord Jesus is an ex officio
    participant in every detail of your family.
    Make sure He always feels at home and
    comfortable with what's going on.

chapter two

FINE-TUNING OUR IDEA OF GREATNESS

One date in recent history permanently seared its mark onto America's conscience: September 11, 2001. This defining moment exposed the best and the worst things about us. It forced us to look in the mirror as a nation and ask ourselves what really matters.

The terrorists who slammed airplanes into the World Trade Center caught us completely off guard. In the middle of a business-as-usual morning, they showed us how naive we were about the magnitude of their hate and the extent to which we could be humbled by their violence.

Many successful people found themselves trapped in the clutches of this ghastly event. At 9:03 that Tuesday morning, their SAT scores and the cars they drove to work meant nothing. There was very little that their pedigrees and résumés could do for them. The famous as well as the obscure became equals in the statistics. In the Twin Towers, "Who's Who" died side by side with "Who's he?"

But in the midst of this crisis, there were magnificent people who responded to the urgency of the moment and gave every-thing they had for the sake of others. As the *successful* rushed down the stairs of the World Trade Center, the *truly great* ran up. As the well-heeled and comfortable ran for their lives, the truly great slipped inside the nightmare to see what they could do to help those who were left behind.

And after the smoke cleared, thousands of truly great people stepped out from their quiet positions within the ranks of successful Americans and opened their hearts and their wallets to those whose lives had been shattered by this cataclysmic event.

Isn't it ironic that as a nation we worship those who are successful, but when tragedy strikes, our survival depends upon those who are great? A cry for help is always answered first by people who live for something more valuable than their own fame or fortune. They respond even though there isn't a thing in it for them.

> Truly great people seldom simply *happen*; they are carefully groomed for the moment long before they are forced to face it.

That's why, when it's time to bury our dead, we mourn the loss of those who were successful, but we celebrate the memory of those who were truly great—the firefighters, the EMTs, the rescue workers, and the countless civilians who sacrificed everything they had for people they'd never met.

Truly great people seldom simply *happen*; they are carefully groomed for the moment long before they are forced to face it. Long before they get to these challenges, so many of them have lived within the proving grounds of a family that inspired them to true greatness.

Uncorrupted Love

As parents, what truly matters more to us than our kids? Sure, we get our schedules out of balance and occasionally spend more time in the office or on the tee box than a conscientious parent should. We get cranky with our kids when we should calm down, and we overreact when we should lighten up.

And let's not fool ourselves: few people annoy us more than our own children. They know which buttons to push to bring out the worst in us. Their music drives us nuts. Their clothing makes us cringe. And their incessant text messaging and IM'ing make us long for the bygone days of smoke signals.

It's hard not to think that children are perhaps a little joke that God is playing on us—especially when they are teenagers. They are God's way of getting us to recognize what He has to put up with in His relationship with us. He says, in effect, "Let me see if I have this right. You created people in your own image who deny you even exist? How's that *feel*?" But, just like God, we wouldn't hesitate to give our lives for our children if it ever came down to it.

That's because there's a place deep down inside a mom and dad's heart that harbors an uncorrupted love. It's that raw material type of love that only wants the best for someone. Like when you stop by your children's rooms at night to cover them up and stand next to their beds, watching them sleep peacefully.

Or when you listen to one side of a phone conversation and realize that the boyfriend or girlfriend on the other end is telling your child that the relationship is over.

Or when your son is lying on a football field, unable to get

> If you aim your children at anything less than greatness, you'll set them up to miss the whole point of their lives.

up after a play, or your daughter has a fever that keeps her from lifting her head off the pillow.

Uncorrupted love only wants to do the right thing, regardless of the price tag that comes with it. It is this type of love I'm appealing to in this book. You have it in you. That's one of the reasons you picked up this book in the first place. This is the kind of love that makes parents want what is best for their children even if it isn't what is best for them.

This is the type of love that compels parents to raise their children for true greatness. I'm going to ask you to call on this love as we delve into this subject together. There's a big reason for this. You see, true greatness isn't always what you think it is. You might even find at times that it isn't what you want it to be. But if you aim your children at anything less than greatness, you'll set them up to miss the whole point of their lives.

Trust me; you don't want to do that.

But if you instill in them this higher calling, this bigger-than-life reason for existing, you'll do something for your children that will outlive you, something that will guarantee that their lives will make a profound difference.

Meet the Parents

Americans have a bad habit of assuming that parents have to have a lot going for them to even come close to raising kids who achieve success, let alone true greatness. If we don't have

the head start of a fortunate pedigree and a nice résumé, we figure that our children simply don't have much of a chance.

Perhaps a visit to a couple of homes might give you a feel for
the kinds of parents God calls on to raise great kids. Let's start
with introductions. There are three couples I'm eager for you to
meet. If you were to grade them based solely on their potential,
they would be average at best. But they took their responsibility as parents seriously, paid attention as they went, and put
forth a stellar effort. Each couple desired something better for
their children than what their own lives had to offer.

Couple #1

The first couple were an ethnic team trying to raise their kids
in a climate of intolerance. They were the minority in a community of bigots. They were the economically disenfranchised
in a society of the upper class. They were part of the religious
underground in a city of spiritual elitism.

When their son was born, they figured he'd have to learn
how to fight hard if he ever wanted to make it to adulthood in
one piece. The only other alternative would be that perhaps the
butterfly of providence would decide to land on his shoulder.
They prepared for the former while praying hard for the latter.
As it turned out, the butterfly not only landed on their son; it
decided to rest on him throughout his childhood.

You've heard these stories before: a gold-guild family from
Nob Hill takes pity on a child from the wrong side of the
tracks. Whether the motive of the wealthy family is guilt or pity
doesn't matter to the impoverished child on the receiving end
of their kindness. For this boy, the gifts he received put him in
the passing lane on the road to success.

It was as though the boy grew up in the wealthy family's home. He ate more meals at their dinner table than he did at his own, and he had carte blanche to the privileges of their lifestyle. Whether it was the swimming pool, the refrigerator, or the remote control, their house was his house; their blessings were his blessings.

His benefactors knew that the boy didn't have a chance at an elite education—not from his parents. So they took it upon themselves to make it happen. They sent him to the best institutions and the finest tutors. When the transformation was complete, you'd never know that this was the same boy who took his first breath in a lean-to in Shantytown. He went from the projects to privilege, from Hamburger Helper to escargot, from tap water to Evian, from the bottom of the food chain to the top of the heap.

Though the wealthy family gave him a lot of amenities, the boy's mom and dad worked to give his life meaning. They prayed throughout his childhood that even though his taste buds had become upper class, his feet would stay planted firmly on common ground. They didn't hesitate to remind him of his roots—a heritage worth celebrating in spite of its minority status.

He paid them back with ambiguity and mixed loyalties. There was an ongoing tension between where he was from and where he had arrived—a tension that he often handled poorly. Maybe he felt guilty about how easy he had it compared to his other family members. Perhaps he struggled to reconcile his birthright with his undeserved blessings. Who knows? Regardless, he often became angry when confronted with the obvious disconnect between who he was and who he had become.

His temper got the best of him one day. The boxing lessons and martial-arts training he received exploded in a sudden rage. When the dust cleared, his opponent was dead. He took off running and never looked back. There were no good-byes to his mom and dad, no thank-yous to his benefactors. Just a lot of miles separating him from what once was and what could have been.

To keep his past from becoming part of his present, he assumed a life of anonymity. He couldn't drop names or flaunt his résumé—he'd have to answer too many questions. Instead, he ended up doing maximum work for minimum wage. He took a cultured childhood and squandered it on a bankrupt career. His parents' dream of their son's great future ended up lying dormant at the end of a road to nowhere.

Couple #2

If you want to experience one of the most gnawing pains a couple can feel, try infertility for a couple of years—or decades. Empty arms. Empty laps. A basket filled with children's books and no one to read them to. Dinners eaten in silence as you both stare at a high chair that remains unexplainably vacant.

This couple knew that pain. They'd gone to all of the specialists, read all the books, and even tried some of the old wives' tales. But the home pregnancy tests remained the same. The rabbit kept on living, even as their expectations kept on dying.

There was only one thing they felt they had going for them—prayer. To them, prayer was classic hope followed by a confident "amen." And they turned to this hope daily. They were as passionate about their prayers to conceive as they were about their physical efforts required to make a baby a reality.

And then—*decades* later—it happened. When the majority of their friends were entering grandparenthood, this couple placed their firstborn on their laps for the first time.

No two people desired to raise a truly great child like this mom and dad. For a son who had been anticipated for so long, a lifestyle of mediocrity and maintaining the status quo simply would not do. That's why they toiled so much to pour every bit of their hopes and dreams into him. They gave him more than just a good education and a cultured lifestyle; they wanted him to be truly extraordinary.

So what did they get for their efforts? They got a kid who stood out in the crowd. Unfortunately, he stood out in ways that his parents would have preferred he didn't. From the eccentric clothes he wore to his unruly hair, this son for whom they had prayed so hard made himself a public spectacle. And then, as though his Bohemian lifestyle wasn't enough, he spent the bulk of his days criticizing popular opinion. He became the blogger of choice for a handful of people who felt that culture had lost its way.

He wasn't above making it personal. In a short period of time, he turned into a professional busybody, pointing out everything wrong with society. His intentions might have been noble, but they were grating nonetheless. And then he stepped over the line. He criticized the man occupying the nearby Oval Office, and the local police interpreted his words as a genuine threat. At the prime of his life, this boy who had been raised to be someone special found himself on the wrong side of prison bars—a surprising outcome for a man whose parents had groomed him so carefully for true greatness.

But surely there's more to the story?

Couple #3

Our third couple got off to a rough start in their life as husband and wife. That's because they had to begin their marriage as Mom and Dad too.

They certainly hadn't planned for their life together to start this way. Who does? He took a liking to her while she was still fairly young. She was the classic "girl next door"; he was the definition of "everyman." Theirs was a romance destined for a marriage made in heaven. They planned to have a conventional wedding, followed by a classical marriage.

But it wasn't to be.

They were high school sweethearts when she got pregnant. It happens sometimes, even to the best of kids. One thing leads to another, and a predictable future is permanently altered.

Did I mention that the baby wasn't his? It was a brief encounter with a secret admirer that happened to leave her in a "family way." It wasn't the first time that a girl with an engagement ring found herself pregnant. But it was one of the rare times when the baby didn't belong to the man who put the ring on her finger.

Scandal. Outrage. Broken promises. A broken heart. These all had to be processed by the young man who had looked forward to the day he'd make this girl his bride. Most guys would have called off the wedding on the spot. Canceling weddings, however, isn't always as easy as abandoning genuine love. Especially when that love runs deeper than the pain of the moment and stands stronger than the contrary pull of public opinion.

In spite of all the reasons he should have said, "I won't," he went ahead and said, "I do." Eventually, they had children of their own. They did their best to make the most of the "yours" and "ours" configuration of their family. They both longed for true greatness for all of their children, even the one who didn't share the father's DNA.

And then, just when a father is supposed to be putting the finishing touches on kids on the front side of adulthood, this father's story ended abruptly. His influence was relegated to memories. And those finishing touches were left on the checklist of a single mom.

Undaunted, this woman went on to finish the job she and her husband had begun. The finishing touches were applied, the final lessons were taught, and the concluding principles of life were whispered in her children's ears.

When the time finally came, the oldest child made his move. His parents had raised him for greatness. Time would now tell if their efforts would pay off.

He hit the ground running. His education and training aligned perfectly with what he felt was his calling. He was a philosopher, a historian, and a ripping good storyteller. He planned to hit the speaking circuit with a message tailor-made for a brave new world. His booking agent was shrewd. The right gigs on the right platforms created an early buzz.

Soon after he began building his speaking career, people all over started to sense that something extraordinary was happening, and they chose to line up with his message. He wanted to create a new way of doing life. His ideas were long overdue and desperately needed. He didn't want to renovate people's lives; he wanted to transform them.

Ah, but idealists tend to be bad for business. This man's ideas posed a serious threat to the political, religious, and social power brokers who surrounded him. So they framed him.

You can do that when you control the media and you've got the police and the local judges on your payroll. In fact, corrupted power can turn public opinion on a dime. It sure did for this widow's son. One day, this young idealist was right on message; the next day he could barely find a dozen people who would give him the time of day.

It got ugly before it got over. In fact, it got downright deadly. The single mom who had poured so much into the heart of her boy was there when he took his last breath. All that she had prayed for, hoped for, and worked for was silenced in the final shudder of his broken-down life.

So what do you think—were these three couples successful in raising their kids? Let's take a closer look.

Taking an Inventory

These three sets of parents worked overtime to raise their kids for true greatness. The first couple, the minority pair, watched their son squander a privileged childhood into a life on the lam. The couple who prayed through the pain of infertility saw their precious boy posing for mug shots. And the young mother who had to get married watched her son end up a sacrifice for what most observers considered a lost cause. So how do you think they did in their attempts to raise their kids for greatness?

Depending on what you believe, you may get a chance to ask them for yourself. The boy who let his anger get the best of him returned home to lead his oppressed minority community to freedom. The world knows him by one name: Moses.

The man with the wild hair who rubbed the powers that be

the wrong way was a forerunner of the King of kings. His nick-name was John the Baptist.

And the young couple who were pregnant when they got married got to have the Savior of the world at their dinner table through His childhood. And His name changed the course of history forever.

You tell me: were these parents aiming their children in the same direction that most parents aim theirs? Even though these three sons were well educated, articulate, and confident, do you think that their parents appraised their value by the kind of grades they made in school, the kind of statistics they put up in Little League baseball or Pop Warner football (they had their equivalents back then), or their popularity level among their peer group? Do you think they emphasized to their sons how important it is to grow up to make a lot of money and wield a lot of power?

These men were known as some of the humblest men of their times, but none of them was a pushover. Jesus, of course, stands apart from them as the perfect God-man. But the questions still have great merit. Do you think these parents embraced the same types of success goals that contemporary Western parents embrace?

Of course not. Their goals for their children weren't even in the same galaxy as most parents' goals. The fact is that most parents prefer that their children blend in rather than stick out. They want their kids to be led through life by their potential rather than their passions. They'd vote for the path of least resistance over the road less traveled.

But there are too many people living in bondage who need a deliverer. Too many people living in darkness who need to see a great light. Too many people living in a lost condition who need to be redeemed.

God may not be calling us to raise a mini-Moses or junior John the Baptist, but He is calling us to raise kids in such a way that they rise to the top when things are sinking to the bottom and move to the front when everyone else is heading for the exit.

The world doesn't remember the people who discuss needs; they remember the people who do something about them. They don't pay tribute to the ones who feel fear; they applaud the ones who stare it down.

We are called to love God so much that we automatically care for people. It's the best way to make sure that when it's time to carry out our mission, bring out the best in our mate, or submit to our master, we neither falter nor flinch. Truly great people rise to these challenges. That's why we'd all do well as parents to keep that bar high *all of the time*.

The world is the unending narrative of a human struggle for meaning, purpose, and hope. Few people get the answers they need to process these pressures. Successful people at least enjoy the luxury of being able to rise above some of these threats and can afford to ignore the impact they have on others. Truly great people would never want to escape from their responsibility to the greater good of the human race.

That's why we need to take notes from people like Moses's parents, Amram and Jochebed; John's folks, Elizabeth and Zacharias; and Jesus's wonderful mom and dad, Mary and Joseph. They raised their sons to be significant rather than successful, and as a result, the world cannot forget their kids' names. But the wealthy and powerful of their time? They've been quickly forgotten. Can you name the pharaoh who raised

> The successful come, achieve, and then leave. The truly great touch people's lives in such a way that their impact lasts forever.

Moses in his palace or the one who chased him out of town? (Thutmose III and Amunhotep II, respectively.) How about the ruler who thought he could silence John the Baptist's voice by taking his life? (Herod Antipas.)

The successful come, achieve, and then leave. The truly great touch people's lives in such a way that their impact lasts forever.

God wants you to play the lead role in empowering your kids to impact the world as these men did. All you have to do is take God's hand and let Him empower you to show them what true greatness looks like.

Ten Ways to Be a
Great Employee (For Parents)

1. Make a commitment to love your fellow workers—especially the ones who are difficult to love.
2. Realize that your attitude toward your job is influencing the way your kids view work as well as the way they view you as a person. Be grateful for your job, and always speak well of the opportunity you have been given to earn a living.
3. Show respect and honor for your employer, supervisors, directors, and immediate bosses. Always speak well of them and to them.
4. If you make a mistake or fall short of expectations, admit it immediately. Never hide behind excuses or pass blame to a fellow employee, even when you've failed badly.
5. Never steal ideas. Be quick to give credit to the source.
6. As much as possible, participate in office social functions. Be a team player inside as well as outside the work arena.
7. Encourage fellow employees who are struggling. To the degree that it is within your power, do whatever you can to help them succeed.

8. Refuse to be part of office gossip about supervisors or fellow employees. Remember, if you help take people down, ultimately, you go down with them.

9. Never take a single thing from the office that belongs to the company (not a paper clip, pencil, stamp, or piece of paper). If your company is generous on these matters, still ask the person in authority if it's all right, and insist on paying for it. Give back more than you are given. Always turn in accurate and absolutely honest expense accounts.

10. Work hard to improve your position in the company. In the meantime, don't complain about your pay. Trust God to see to it that you are fairly dealt with on payday.

chapter three

THE SUCCESS ILLUSION

D an wasn't the slowest man alive, but he was going to give the guy who *was* a run for his money. He was congregating with a bunch of other runners just outside Kyle Field at Texas A&M University, stretching his muscles in preparation for a 5K race. The world-class runners would be at the front of the pack. Dan was more than happy to take his place somewhere among the rear guard. He was there to prove to himself that he could run five kilometers and still live to tell about it.

I've known Dan for a long time. If anyone has grasped the essence of true greatness, it's this humble and unassuming man. Don't think, however, that his humility has cost him when it comes to success. In every way the world measures success, Dan is at the top of the heap. He just didn't live his life with success as his goal. His success was simply a by-product of his steady commitment to live for something bigger than what he could get out of life. Fortunately as well as unfortunately, his desire to focus on true greatness came in handy sooner than he would have wanted in his life.

Dan and his wife, Caye, got a crash course in what really matters in life shortly after the birth of their first child—a gentle wind named Catie. When Catie was three, she was diagnosed with leukemia. When she was eight, it claimed her life. In between, all of the priorities that most success-oriented parents focus on showed themselves for what they truly were: empty, useless, and nothing.

There was no positioning for favoritism within her school or groping for popularity among her friends. There was no fretting over which preschool would be the perfect springboard into the best Title I university. Instead, Dan and Caye showed their daughter what a passionate love for God and an unquenchable concern for others looks like. By the time she was at the height of her fight with cancer, Catie was already a card-carrying member of the truly great.

I remember when I got the call that Catie had slipped from the grasp of time and space. That precious girl had already shined more for God and lived more for others than most people do in a lifetime. And I'm not exaggerating for the sake of the memory of a sweet little girl. If you had been at Catie's funeral and asked to speak with people who could testify to this girl's amazing love, the line would have been long and the stories would have kept coming. Catie's friends and their parents were made better by the brief life of this unpretentious girl.

Dan and Caye prove that you don't need a lot of time to make a difference in your kid's life; you just have to be deliberate. But when you extend that deliberateness throughout an entire childhood, there is no stopping the potential that you can harness in your children.

Dan and Caye prove this even more in the incredible job they have done of raising their other daughter. She's brilliant and beautiful and has talent that goes off of the charts. She's at an Ivy League school, not because she needed it, but because it needed her. She is already successful and will easily transfer this success into an enviable life without even trying. That's because she *isn't* trying. Success, as this world defines it, would be far too puny a reason for which to live her life. Instead, she's living for the things that will ultimately outlive her. She exists in order to leave a legacy that will never die. When people talk about her, they don't compliment her keen intellect, her incredible gift for playing the cello, or her extraordinary talent as a leader. Instead, they praise her graciousness, kindness, tenderness, and humility.

Which brings me back to Dan at the 5K race. During his warm-up, he couldn't help but notice a large group of runners who had gathered around a Dumpster behind the Aggies' football stadium. Something had grabbed their attention, so Dan moved in for a closer look.

What he found in the Dumpster was a sobering reminder of the things that really matter. For there in that huge, industrial-size garbage can were hundreds of trophies and plaques that had been discarded by the athletic department. These glimmering tributes to success had once been held with pride by athletes who had won them at a great personal price. The moment when they were awarded was special. The reason for their sacrifice was legitimate. But the significance of these awards in the larger scheme of life was irrelevant. Now they were awaiting the truck that would crush them to dust and discard them in a landfill.

Soon the gun sounded, and Dan took his place among the masses of runners making their way toward the finish line five clicks away. But along the way, he found himself wondering how many of his priorities and efforts would someday be thrown into eternity's Dumpster.

The Fastest Man Alive

I know another man, and I wish he had asked himself this bigger-than-life question.

We met him in the introduction to this book. He was known as "the fastest man alive," and he was leaning over the shoulder of my wife with his face down close enough to her cheek that he could take in a full, deep breath of her perfume.

We were on a flight from Dallas to Tampa, sitting in the nice seats toward the front of the plane. Darcy and I had been reading when this man had slipped out of his seat a few rows in front of us, turned around to study her for a moment, and then made his approach. He decided coming up from behind and to the side would work best. He knelt down beside her and softly whispered in her ear, "Hey, beautiful lady, do you know who I am?" Darcy turned to look at her admirer.

The eyes that were only inches from hers were tired, sunken, and yellowed, perhaps from a little too much time leaning against a bar. His face was pleasant enough, but his body looked like its best years were somewhere in the distant past. "The fastest man alive" stood up straight, took a few steps forward, and extended his hand. Darcy reached out and gave it a good, firm shake. "I'm sorry, but I don't recognize you," she said.

He looked sad for a moment. Then he put on an easy smile and said, "Lady, I am the *great* Bobby Hayes."

Darcy looked at me to see if his name rang a bell. I said, "Darcy, this man was one of the finest wide receivers ever to play for the Dallas Cowboys. In fact, he played for them during the time you and I lived there—back when I was in graduate school. We watched him at several of the games we went to."

Bobby was obviously delighted that I recognized his name. He filled in a few of the blanks in his résumé for Darcy and proudly showed her his Super Bowl ring. But it was obvious that his zenith years were in the distant past. The years of physical abuse had done a lot of damage to his height and mobility.

Hayes was only a few years older than me, but he looked old enough to be my grandfather. That's what happens when you have a few too many linebackers spearing their helmets into your side over a period of years. "The Bullet" looked more like a spent casing. "The fastest man alive" looked like he would soon need a walker to make his next move on a pretty lady. I didn't feel challenged by his interest in my wife, and Darcy didn't feel threatened. Actually, we both felt the same thing.

Pity.

Bobby Hayes had once ruled the world of football. But not anymore.

The days of Bobby Hayes, the fastest man alive, the sports icon, the gridiron celebrity, were gone for good. His success now required a few stiff belts of bourbon and a full-on approach to unsuspecting women if he wanted public recognition.

Darcy and I felt that the moment called for us to put down our books and give Mr. Hayes the attention he was craving. It was hard to say how much the liquor was talking, but the more Bobby shared his accomplishments, the sadder and more pathetic he became.

And then he did something that showed how deceptive success can be when it comes to defining oneself. He started telling

Darcy about his crowning achievement at the 1964 Olympics—and then he reached in the pocket of his sports jacket and pulled out the gold medal they had hung around his neck almost forty years earlier.

The ribbon was faded and soiled from decades of frequent handling. As Darcy rested the medal in her hand, she could see that the gold had long since lost its luster. Her eyes walked their way from the medal, up the ribbon, past his hands, and onto the face that seemed to be begging for approval. "That's a beautiful medal, Bobby," Darcy said. "I'm glad I got to meet you in person."

He nodded and smiled. "It was nice to meet the both of you too." He patted her on her shoulder a couple of times, nodded good-bye, and then shuffled past the drawn curtain into the coach section of the plane.

From the other side of the curtain, we heard him say to someone in the first row, "Do you know who I am?"

The Intoxication of Artificial Success

Moments like this encounter with Bobby Hayes remind us how hollow man-made accolades can become. When the cheering of the crowd dies down and the calls from the press dwindle, all you have left is the unvarnished reality of your broken-down life. When your view of yourself is defined by a brief claim to fame in the past, it's not surprising that some people have to resort to these kinds of come-ons to feel as though they still have value. I wonder if any of the plaques and trophies that Bobby earned as a Dallas Cowboy have ended up in a Dumpster behind Texas Stadium.

Darcy and I felt an overwhelming sadness for the "great"

Bobby Hayes. Before the flight was over, Bobby had gone from the front of the coach section to the back, told everyone who would listen about his track record, and showed many people his gold medal. It broke our hearts that this man didn't think we would find him inter-esting unless he had some stellar accomplishment as his calling card. When you live your life for recogni-tion, it's hard to think that anyone would give you the time of day without it.

> When the cheering of the crowd dies down and the calls from the press dwindle, all you've got left is the unvarnished reality of your broken-down life.

We live in a day when success is defined by looks, IQ, strategic alliances, titles, and world records. I could keep the list going for several pages. Success is supposed to attract people's attention and put you in a superior position in the human pecking order. And it is the natural desire average parents have for their children.

This definition of *success* is what overtakes us when we sit down every December to pen the annual letter that will go out with our Christmas cards. We assume that the things that place our children in a league of their own are the things that our friends are longing to hear about. The folded-up sheets of red and green paper often tell the story of a child's head start on the path to success.

I enjoy hearing how my friends are doing and how their kids are faring. But in the process of reading my way through the pile of letters that we receive, it's easy to see that parenting can become preoccupied with crowding a child's academic, athletic, and social résumé with the accolades that count most in our culture but don't have any bearing on eternity.

That's because there is something extremely contagious about the desire for success. When you are bombarded at every television show, every athletic event, and every glance at the celebrity section of the newspaper, it's easy to see how parents could unwittingly think that it might be in their children's best interest to get a piece of the action before it's all over. It's also easy to see why so many parents assume that the world's view of success is something their kids can't live without.

> There is something extremely contagious about the desire for success.

THE SUCCESS ILLUSION

Our kids have to be . . .
. . . the smartest.
. . . the fastest.
. . . the prettiest.
. . . the best connected.
. . . the most popular.
. . . the best outfitted.
. . . the best rewarded.
. . . the most confident.

The Lure of the Success Illusion

Jesus knew all about the lure of success. He was surrounded by people who had swallowed its hook. The Pharisees were the religious and political brokers of his day. Their position afforded them high social status and nice returns on payday. Despite how others viewed the Pharisees, Jesus spent most of His time ignoring them. This, of course, was a response they weren't used to, which caused them to get in His face, demanding more respect. He simply ignored them that much more, but not before He weighed in on their false understanding of true greatness.

Listen to Jesus's harsh indictment of status for status' sake:

> "Watch out for the teachers of the law. They like to walk around in flowing robes and be greeted in the marketplaces, and have the most important seats in the synagogues and the places of honor at banquets. They devour widows' houses and for a show make lengthy prayers. Such men will be punished most severely." (Mark 12:38–40)

Although this did nothing for His popularity in their eyes, Jesus didn't seem to care. He was here to introduce the essence of true greatness by showing us what it looked like through His example. And one thing was certain: the Pharisees didn't have a clue what greatness was.

Jesus even went out of His way to draw a comparison between the success illusion of a Pharisee and the true greatness of someone who has God's heart. You can read it for yourself in Luke 18:9–14:

To some who were confident of their own righteousness and looked down on everybody else, Jesus told this parable: "Two men went up to the temple to pray, one a Pharisee and the other a tax collector. The Pharisee stood up and prayed about himself: 'God, I thank you that I am not like other men—robbers, evildoers, adulterers—or even like this tax collector. I fast twice a week and give a tenth of all I get.'

"But the tax collector stood at a distance. He would not even look up to heaven, but beat his breast and said, 'God, have mercy on me, a sinner.'

"I tell you that this man, rather than the other, went home justified before God. For everyone who exalts himself will be humbled, and he who humbles himself will be exalted."

Whether it was the rich young ruler, a religious lawyer, the high priest, or Pontius Pilate himself, Jesus did not respond to people based on their net worth, titles, or status. Instead, He dealt with them according to the true attitudes of their hearts. This is why so many of these people found themselves looking up to Jesus rather than the other way around.

Unfortunately, many Christian parents miss Jesus's view of greatness and get lost in the maze of the world's passion for success. Everywhere we turn and just about everything we hear people say reminds us that we should be raising kids whose primary goal is to post high marks and great statistics. To them, life is about success that can be quantified in degrees or dollar signs.

We can camouflage these expectations in clever spiritual rhetoric, but in the long run, if we get it wrong, our kids will find themselves propping up empty lives when they're our age.

All because we unwittingly bought into a lie that true greatness has something to do with accomplishments or accoutrements.

Getting Sidetracked

Maybe we'd all be a little better off if we look at the anchor tenets of the success illusion. To make it easier, let me list the most obvious: fame, power, health and beauty, and wealth.

Fame

Fame is an extremely attractive substitute for true greatness. Our culture worships at the altar of celebrity. The more well known you are, the more significant you appear—regardless of how you gained your fame.

But Jesus often calls us to a life of obscurity. He said, "Those who try to keep their lives will lose them. But those who give up their lives will save them" (Luke 17:33 NCV).

The Hall of Fame chapter, Hebrews 11, praises Bible heroes who were great but not well known. These saints "through their faith . . . defeated kingdoms. They did what was right, received God's promises, and shut the mouths of lions. They stopped great fires and were saved from being killed with swords. They were weak, and yet were made strong. . . . The world was not good enough for them!" (Hebrews 11:33–35, 38 NCV).

Which would you rather raise: a child who is famous in the world's eyes but whose fame will fade with time, or a child who grows up so valuable (even in obscurity) that the best that the world has to offer him in reward doesn't even come close to paying him what he is truly worth? I think I can guess your answer. It happens when you raise them for things that matter for eternity.

Let me qualify the fact that celebrity in and of itself is not a wicked thing. It's possible to become well known without pursuing it. Your fame might be the logical result of things you've done well or circumstances that simply came your way. But when celebrity is something you long for and *need*, it's quite a different situation. People who pursue fame for the sake of fame find that it is little more than smoke and mirrors. Even worse, there is no loyalty in celebrity. The paparazzi who work so hard to make you famous take even more delight in tearing you apart.

Without even trying, parents can unwittingly format their children to need the empty praise of fame by orchestrating their lives so that they can become popular among their young peer group. There's a fine line between encouraging our children to excel and pushing them to achieve the public's attention in the process.

Can celebrity be the outcome of true greatness? Of course! To prove this point, you only need two words we brought up in the introduction: Mother Teresa. There is no doubt that this waif of a woman achieved worldwide fame before she died. But she didn't go looking for it; fame found her. The fact is, true greatness often garners attention. But when we keep pushing the dream of fame on our children, we can unwittingly set them up for an adult life of discouragement when the spotlight of celebrity shines on someone else.

I find the timing of Mother Teresa's death quite interesting. She died just a few days after Princess Diana was killed in a car accident in Paris. While the world mourned the British superstar, God slipped this gentle nun out a side door to escape public attention.

Diana was a celebrity born of beauty, wealth, privilege, title, and royalty. She and Mother Teresa were in completely different leagues, and if Princess Diana were here, she'd be the first to admit it. She met the nun from Calcutta and was admittedly in awe of this precious saint's unending compassion. Mother Teresa had a heart filled with overwhelming love for God and unquenchable compassion for others.

Now *that's* what true celebrity should look like!

Power

Power is what you get when you take the desire to influence and put it on a daily diet of relational steroids. There are some parents who think they must raise their children to rule the world. They push them to be first, to take charge, and to assume the top position. "You're the best!" "There is no one in your league!" "Don't let anyone get in your way!" "Show no mercy!" "Take no prisoners!"

Jesus's half brother James counters this mind-set. He says, "Don't be too proud in the Lord's presence, and he will make you great" (James 4:10 NCV).

There is no doubt that power can give you a rush. The fact that you are in control, that no one can overwhelm you, and that people are at your mercy—well, it's a road trip fit for a king. But unless you happen to be a king, it is also a trap for fools. Power for power's sake seldom turns out well.

Our culture is intoxicated with power. The need to dominate and control is part of our self-protective inner being. There is a normal amount of give-and-take in any relationship, but some people feel that the only way to excel is to put others in a position of submission to them and to keep them there.

The marketplace is crowded with Barney Fifes—people with too little ability in positions of too much authority (remember the bullet he kept in his shirt pocket?). High controllers bring out the worst in the people close to them. That's why indoctrinating your children into needing to rule people sets them up for a lot of heartache.

Let's keep in mind, of course, that many kids pop out of their mother's womb hardwired to dominate. They proceed to take over the daily agenda of the house with their powerful lungs and their determined wills. These kids are *gifts* from God. You are getting to train a leader. But if these children aren't raised in submission to the

> True greatness does not have power as its goal, but it often gains power by default.

leadership of their parents, and if they don't have the essence of true greatness instilled into them, they can grow up to do a lot of damage. If you don't have a plan to point them toward true greatness, they'll most likely practice their high-controlling techniques on you before they get out on their own.

True greatness does not have power as its goal, but it often gains power by default. As we shall see, this higher goal of parenting often gives your children incredible authority when they are adults. Unfortunately, society is enamored by the world's quest for control, and parents often take pride when their kids desire to dominate and subjugate all the players in their future.[1]

Health and Beauty

Given the choice of feeling my tip-top best or physically lousy all the time, there is no debate: I choose health. The same goes for physical fitness.

There's nothing wrong with wanting to stay in good shape. In fact, taking care of our bodies is a reflection of our stewardship to God. He created our bodies, and He joins us in living there through the Holy Spirit. The least we can do is keep the house we're both occupying in good repair.

And there is nothing wrong with wanting to look your best. That attitude comes from God too. He creates the desire within us to want to put our best faces forward. Health, fitness, and attractiveness are all legitimate parts of a vigorous spiritual life.

The problem comes when we deify and worship health and beauty. This happens when our view of ourselves doesn't come from our relationship with God but from the way we fit into our clothes and the images looking back at us in the mirror each morning. Our need for superior health makes it tough for us to be sick or injured. Our moods become the sock puppet of how we feel physically at any given moment. We find it too difficult to maintain good attitudes and treat people kindly when we aren't feeling well.

The bigger problem comes with the artificial value we place on ourselves and others if we (or they) happen to hit a higher aesthetic standard of personal beauty than the average person. It's subtle, but people who need beauty to feel complete often give "beautiful people" far more influence than they genuinely have, are far more lenient with them than they deserve, and assume they are far more successful than they actually are.

The rows and rows of magazines devoted to the lives of the beautiful people demonstrate how pervasive this attitude is. Often, all you're seeing in those magazines are the people who have the most free time to spend at the gym and the most money to spend at the dentist and plastic surgeon's office.

Deifying health and beauty makes it very difficult to grow old, especially for women. There's also a direct threat to the intimacy in marriage relationships when men and women put unrealistic emphasis on health and beauty.

Perhaps the greatest tragedy is what happens to plain, sickly, or overweight children who grow up in homes with parents who are overly fixated on health and beauty. These children know that they will never measure up. It is next to impossible for these children to feel good about themselves when their parents assume that great health, physical fitness, and striking good looks make you a better person or are necessary to achieve success.

Wealth

There is absolutely nothing wrong with making a comfortable living or having more money than you need. For most people, acquiring wealth is simply the result of conscientious choices they've made in developing their gifts and skills. With that said, wealth still ends up on the list of priorities when it comes to people's view of success. Of all the false gods masquerading as greatness, money heads the list. And when you leaf back through the other nominees, you see that they are simply side roads that lead to this one.

There are very few parents who wouldn't list near the top of their parenting priorities the need to equip their children to make a good living. Money is so important to many parents that it is not uncommon for a mom or dad to push a child to pursue a certain vocation simply because of its income potential. Whether the child has an aptitude for it, or even enjoys it, is irrelevant. The important thing is that he spends his adult life doing something that *pays well*.

> We must be careful to avoid equating wealth with greatness. They are not the same.

But wealth, by itself, is just money; nothing more. It doesn't make you better or smarter or kinder. It just gives you a few more options in life. The world is crowded with people who have more money than they know what to do with but are miserable.

My personal hope for your children is that they grow up to be able to create all the income they need to carry out their greater purposes in life. I would even desire that they end up with more than they need. But we must be careful to avoid equating wealth with greatness. They are not the same.

September 18, 2002

Darcy and I were cleaning up from dinner and listening to the news on television when the announcer came back from a commercial break with these words: "Bobby Hayes, Olympic track marvel and celebrated wide receiver of the Dallas Cowboys, died today of kidney failure." He spent a few seconds recapping the highlights of his athletic career. He closed by saying, "The great Bobby Hayes, the fastest man alive, dead at the age of fifty-nine."

Darcy and I remembered the broken-down man we met on the flight to Tampa. We thought about how desperate he seemed to be to get our attention and gain our approval. It reminded us again what an empty shell man-made success can be.

As we have seen, true greatness isn't about fame, power, beauty, or wealth. It's about a passionate love for God that demonstrates itself in an unquenchable love and concern for others.

Ten Ways to Build a Great Attitude in Your Kids' Hearts Toward God

1. Have a joyful faith. Believe big. Trust huge. Let your children see a belief in God that makes you a much happier and more agreeable person to live with.

2. Be actively involved in a thriving church. Find a church that exudes a mighty joy and an exciting attitude toward God.

3. No matter what church you go to, refuse to criticize the people who serve you. Love your pastor, worship leader, youth workers, Sunday school teachers, and volunteers. If there is a legitimate concern, deal with the person face-to-face in a spirit of grace, love, and kindness. Anything short of that, and we become the real problem.

4. Do not speak unkindly about your church, or people who serve in the church, around your children. The church is Jesus's bride, and if we insult the church, we insult the Lord. Also, bitter talk and a critical spirit make us a pawn in Satan's hand.

5. Pray for the people who serve your church.

6. Pull your weight. Volunteer your time, your spiritual gifts, and your sweat to carry the burden of service of your church. Sign up to

work in the nursery and Sunday school program. Remember: it's not about us.

7. Set the example for your children by consistently supporting your church financially.

8. If the worship is getting too loud and too
   enthusiastic for you, bring some tissue for
   your ears, smile, worship your heart out, and
   be excited for the new generation of believ-
   ers who are being ministered to. Once again:
   it's not about us.

9. Decide once and for all that you love God's
   Word. Make it a daily part of your routine.
   When you pray, lift up each one of your children and grandchildren by name . . . every
   day. Let your kids find God's Word in your lap
   and His love in your heart.

10. Bring your family to church every Sunday,
    and encourage them during the week. Pray
    with them and for them. Minister to your
    children's hearts throughout the week so
    that they can show up for church ready to
    love God and love others.

chapter four

THE PARADOX OF TRUE GREATNESS

Several years ago, I was trying to help a father reconnect with his son. Father and son were part of a family that worshiped success. Everything they had, they had in abundance, and everything they did was first-class. The father built high-end homes. He knew how to indulge his son; he just didn't know how to enfold him into his heart. As the boy moved into his teenage years, he drew a distinct line between himself and his dad.

This was also a Christian home. Mom and Dad were deliberate about their faith and took an active role in trying to keep Jesus front and center in their daily family life. But they made a technical error that many Christians make: they ran the Bible through their success filters rather than running their view of success through the filter of the Bible. And the results put a chill on their worldview.

It was during a trip through one of the dad's building projects that I saw why these parents—and especially the father—had lost contact with their boy's heart.

The three of us were driving by a section of unfinished houses. Dad was behind the wheel and serving as tour guide. I was in the front passenger seat. The prodigal son was sitting in the back, working hard to balance the chip on his shoulder. As we slowly drove down the street, a laborer came out of the front door of one of the houses and walked over to a pile of bricks next to a cement mixer. A bricklaying crew was inside, constructing a fireplace. The laborer was keeping them supplied with materials.

My friend pulled his car to a stop, and we sat there watching the man make two stacks of bricks and then carefully pick them up under his arms. His skin was weathered, and his hands were callused from years of manual toil. He nodded to us and then proceeded to carry the bricks into the house for the bricklayers.

Dad broke the silence with pointed words directed at his son: "You see that? At the rate you are going, that's how you are going to end up. If you don't change your ways, you're going to find yourself at the bottom of the food chain, just like that old man, wasting his life and barely making minimum wage." He winked at me, as if to say, "There! I just gave him a good taste of reality."

I didn't say anything. I wanted to wait until the father and I were alone. When we finally got back to their home, the boy headed straight into the house.

I didn't hesitate. "Why on earth did you make that ridiculous remark about that laborer back there?" I asked the father.

"What are you talking about? What ridiculous remark?" The father had no clue what I was talking about.

"Are you nuts? You disparaged a perfectly good man doing a perfectly respectable job," I countered. "That man is working hard and doing a service for *you*. Why would you devalue him and his role simply because it is a minimum-wage job? What that man does and what he makes isn't a statement of his personal worth. How do you know what kind of man he is? For all we know, he might have more heart and more character than you and me combined."

The father just stood there with his mouth agape. Apparently, he wasn't used to friends talking to him like this. And he clearly hadn't thought of the greater ramifications of his words.

Proverbs 27:6 says, "The slap of a friend can be trusted to help you, but the kisses of an enemy are nothing but lies" (NCV). It would have been easier for me just to tell this man what he wanted to hear, but I wouldn't have been much of a friend if I had. I've learned that you never get very far surrounded by a bunch of "yes" people. My closest friends tell me what I need to hear rather than what I want to hear. And this man needed a real friend telling him the truth rather than standing safely on the side while he destroyed what little relationship he had left with his son.

We had a great conversation about shallow values. It was part of the reason he and his son were growing so far apart. The boy could see that his father placed a higher priority on worldly success than he did on the higher calling of a humble and gracious spirit before God. Their comfortable Christian lifestyle was a by-product of his father's desire to have wealth and to enjoy the safe distance it afforded them from the concerns and needs of the people around them.

The success syndrome had subtly programmed this man's theology and worldview. Although the father was right to be concerned about the direction his son's life was taking, his preoccupation with the trappings of success caused him to draw wrong conclusions when it came to redirecting his son. He sabotaged his influence on his son by allowing success to pollute him with arrogance. The boy could see the disconnection between what his father said and what he was supposed to believe, and it caused him to want to reject both his father and his father's faith.

In time, this father came around. Fortunately, so did his son. But not before the boy had hit the brick walls at the end of several emotional and moral dead ends.

The Usual Suspects

In the previous chapter, we marched out the usual suspects that parents assume lead their kids to a life of success: fame, power, beauty, and wealth. But we saw that these things run counter to the qualities that God's Word says really matter. They have no connection to a child who wants to surrender to a life of true greatness.

Like the father and son we just observed, the Western culture's view of success can block a well-intended Christian family from seeing the bigger and far nobler picture of what God says is important.

I saw this played out many years ago at the expense of a girl who could have been raised for true greatness. When I was a kid, a family left our church because their daughter didn't get elected president of the youth group. Let's lay aside the whole issue of whether youth groups should be electing officers and focus on the bigger issue—why would someone determine their faithfulness to church based on the outcome of a popularity contest?

Church isn't about accolades that we receive but about worship that we offer. It's not about prestige for the participants but about gracious service to the saints. Our attitude toward doing the work of God's ministry in our church should be to do whatever we can, forget who gets credit for it, and pray that God gets all the glory.

The girl was disappointed. Her parents, however, were incensed. Somehow, their view of the Christian life had no room for playing the role of an also-ran. So they gathered up their Bibles and went looking for a "friendlier" church.

What possible good could come out of salving their bruised egos by leaving the church? Their overreaction to the situation demonstrated for their daughter what their faith looked like under pressure.

The fragile faith of many adult parishioners sets their children up to reject their parents' faith. Just like the son who received mixed messages from his success-driven father in the housing project, children can't help but question the authenticity of their parents' faith. They ask themselves, "If this is what following Jesus actually looks like, who needs it?"

That's the question this girl ultimately asked. By the time she graduated from high school, she had abandoned many of the values that our church and her youth leader could have helped her embrace. But when you evaluated her actions against the priorities of her parents, it all added up.

God doesn't add the way we do. In His divine economy, low equals high, patient equals aggressive, small equals big, and anonymity equals renown. When parents figure this out, they don't make demeaning value judgments about people who don't make much money, and they couldn't care less whether their children receive man-made accolades at the expense of a greater good.

Darcy and I saw this conflict very close to home. Recognition for a job well done caught our son in a crossfire between the illusion of success and the priorities of true greatness. Because of his excellent academic efforts, he was inducted into the National Honor Society.

The problem came when the school adviser explained the conditions of membership. In order to claim his position among this elite and commendable group, he had to regularly attend their meetings and participate in their service projects. There was one big problem: their meetings were on Monday evenings. But our son already had a commitment on Monday evenings—he volunteered in an inner-city ministry that helped poor, disenfranchised kids, many of whom depended on his involvement to lighten the load they carried through life. It wasn't even a tough decision. He simply ignored the opportunity to be a member in good standing of the National Honor Society because it didn't fit in with the commitment he had made to others in greater need.

His academic counselor at school questioned his decision to pass up a vital role in the school's NHS guild. As she explained to him, he would not be able to wear the special sash that set him apart as a member of the National Honor Society at his graduation, and his inactive status would mean he couldn't list the honor society on his résumé when he applied for college. When he asked whether the meeting could be moved to a different evening or whether he could attend a chapter at another school, he was told that these options were out of the question.

But for our son, if anything was "out of the question," it was the thought of turning his back on the opportunity he had to be part of an active mission to hurting children. I couldn't agree more with his decision.

I even had to endure some grief from a friend who worked as a career counselor in our school system. He felt that by backing up our son's decision, we were undermining his future academic success. When I explained that his future success was far more connected to his character, I was rebuffed as though I had no clue what it took to get into a prestigious school. He couldn't see the simple truth that true greatness finds no home in a life that is focused only on the trappings of success.

For the record, my son attended a prestigious university. This story has the same happy ending of many others. When we choose the higher ground, success often gets thrown in. One of the things the admissions department of this school was impressed with on his application was the fact that he served in the inner city throughout his years in high school. During the application process, he spared them the sad story about sacrificing his status in the National Honor Society.

Let's Make a Deal

Do you remember the game show *Let's Make a Deal*? It was one of those mind-numbing shows that your intellect told you not to watch because it was "below" you, but you watched it anyway. I always thought it was high entertainment (which puts the true extent of my intellect into proper perspective). In the show, contestants would be given an option: they could either have what was under the small cardboard box in front of them or whatever was behind . . . Door #2. Depending on how they chose, they'd get either a new car or a can of fruit cocktail.

When the choice was between a door that could conceal something big and a box that could only hold something small, most people went for the door. Obviously, the creators of the show knew that the average person assumes that bigger is better, so they weren't opposed to putting the keys to the car in the small box and the can of fruit cocktail on the floor behind the huge door. This classic game show played off people's greed and their desire to get ahead in life without having to do much work to get there.

There's a bit of a game of *Let's Make a Deal* going on in the tension between success and true greatness. Success offers us all of the benefits that come with fame, power, beauty, and wealth. It appeals to our lusts, our moods, our fears, and our inadequacies.

Then true greatness comes along and offers us the treasure it has for us behind its doors. Things like these:

○ a clear knowledge of how bankrupt we are spiritually
○ sadness and mourning
○ meekness and humility
○ hunger and thirst

So let's see: we could have fame, or we could be obscure with meekness thrown into the mix to make things more interesting. We could have wealth, or we could realize how spiritually penniless we are. We could have power, or we could have righteous cravings that gnaw away at us. Man, these are difficult decisions!

It's no wonder that we find ourselves drawn to the lure of success. True greatness looks awful at first glance. But we must keep in mind that God doesn't do the math the same way we do. He has a different economy than the world has. When we understand how He's adding everything up, it's not only easier to cast our lot with true greatness, but it's also much more desirable.

The Sermon on the Mount

In His Sermon on the Mount, Jesus gives us an overview of what it's like to hand our hearts over to the God of the universe and the King of kings. The cause and effect works something like this: when you truly understand what God has done for you, it's hard to resist wanting to live on His behalf, to run every opportunity that crosses your path through a "kingdom" filter.

In the opening verses of this discourse, we get a preview of this divine economy. In these verses, Jesus outlines a series of paradoxes that point to the rich reward of true greatness.

The back-door purpose of the Sermon on the Mount is to remind us that when it comes to God's economy, He says, "My thoughts are not your thoughts, neither are your ways my ways" (Isaiah 55:8). People who have a passionate love for God show it in the way they live for His glory and use their lives to point others toward Him.

Using Matthew 5:3–10 as our focal point, let's take a look at a few of the verses of this sermon to see what kind of a sum Jesus comes up with when He adds all of His priorities together.

Blessed Are the Poor in Spirit,
for Theirs Is the Kingdom of Heaven

Jesus says that we are in line for God's blessing when we realize that we are morally, emotionally, and spiritually bankrupt—and there is nothing we can do to fix our problem. We don't delude ourselves into thinking that our good works, self-righteousness, strategic contacts, or personal resources can do anything to alter our condition. That's because they can't.

We throw ourselves completely at the mercy of the God who gave His Son to fix our dilemma by dying on the cross. Because we put ourselves completely in His care, we have become citizens of the kingdom of heaven and have every right to start living our lives with this future destination in view.

Blessed Are Those Who Mourn,
for They Will Be Comforted

In light of the fact that God has done such an overwhelming work of grace in our lives, we are more sensitive to the part that our sin played in His death. It grieves us when we realize how much our sin cost Him.

This contrite attitude makes us desire to please Him with our lives. It also makes us more sensitive to the sin that holds in its clutches so many of the people who surround us. Rather than condemn these people, we want the same grace for them that Christ showed to us. We grieve over the pains that they endure, the losses they have to process, and the disappointments that haunt their lives—especially the ones that are the result of their lost condition.

God says, because of this tender attitude, "I'm going to personally comfort you."

Blessed Are the Meek,
for They Will Inherit the Earth

The fact that God, and only God, could save us from ourselves causes us to have a realistic view of who we are and who we aren't. Furthermore, receiving a love that we don't deserve causes us to want to give Him all of the credit. His transforming grace puts us in a position where we not only don't *want* to puff ourselves up, but we don't *need* to. His grace is so sufficient for us that we feel secure enough, significant enough, and strong enough in Him that we are satisfied.

This attitude makes us more valuable to people on earth and makes the earth more enjoyable to us. As David said, "Because the Lord is my Shepherd, what more could I possibly want?" (Psalm 23:1, author's paraphrase). When we don't need all that the earth has to offer, it becomes far more pleasing to live here.

Blessed Are Those Who Hunger and Thirst
for Righteousness, for They Will Be Filled

Because God has so completely satisfied us through His work on our behalf, we don't get hungry or thirsty for the things that used to drive us before we came to know Him—things like recognition, influence, vanity, and material possessions. Instead, we have new taste buds. Our deeper appetite and our demanding thirst are for the things that are true, right, good, and decent. These are the things that benefit us the most, empower the people around us the most, and glorify God the most.

Because of this new appetite and thirst, God supplies us with endless opportunities to satisfy them through the way we love Him in our actions and the opportunities we use to pass on His love to others.

Blessed Are the Merciful,
for They Will Be Shown Mercy

When we didn't have a prayer, God came to our aid with a tender understanding. Since we have received so much mercy, the least we can do is to give it out to everyone we possibly can.

The thing about mercy is that it tends to multiply itself. Kindness begets kindness. Pretty soon, what goes around comes around and washes back over us. It's God's promise to the people who treat others the way He treats them.

Blessed Are the Pure in Heart,
for They Will See God

The cleansing influence of God's grace and the transforming power of His forgiveness have a way of exposing our faulty thinking. Next thing we know, we're thinking God's thoughts. Purity has an uncanny ability to help us see God's goodness and holiness.

They say that the way you know you've mastered a foreign language is when you start to think in that language without first translating it in your mind from your native tongue. When we truly grasp the enormity of God's love for us, grace becomes our new native tongue. God's presence starts to permeate our thought processes.

Next thing we know, we're looking at the world through filters that see what He sees. We start to see His signature on current events, hear His voice slip through the background noise of our busy lives, and feel His arm around our shoulders and His finger pointing the way when we're not sure what to do next.

Blessed Are the Peacemakers, for They Will Be Called Sons of God

Before we experienced God's love, the best we could come up with was being a peacekeeper. We used our minds to outwit the problem and our muscles to keep it under control. But once we got in step with the Savior, He changed the way we dealt with these problems. We became His emissaries for transformed lives. Loving hearts replaced clever minds, and forgiveness replaced our need to rattle our swords.

Bottom line: when people get close to us, they should sense God's reconciling presence in the way we deal with conflict.

Blessed Are Those Who Are Persecuted Because of Righteousness, for Theirs Is the Kingdom of Heaven

Doing the right thing in a culture that often worships doing what's wrong cannot be carried out without paying a price. But because of what God has done for us, the least we can do is put up with a little pushback—or even a lot of it. It's par for the course when you're committed to righteous living in an unrighteous world. Our righteousness might cost us fame, power, money, and even a place at the table with those who worship themselves. We may have to endure some well-placed insults to our ego or some unfortunate disruptions of our comfort zones. But when you compare it to what God has waiting for us in heaven, it's an extremely small price to pay.

Having a realistic view of our spiritual condition, identifying with other people's needs, acknowledging how undeserving we are of God's love, pursuing noble and virtuous goals, giving other people the benefit of the doubt, keeping our motives in line with God's heart, living at peace with the people around us, and being willing to endure antagonism for our faith—these are the things that make up the economy of true greatness. They also trump any reward that success has to offer.

Movers, Shakers, Givers, Takers

It would be nice if we could read God's Word, take it at face value, and live accordingly. Unfortunately for most of us, God needs to get our attention.

That's exactly what He did for a young entrepreneur. The story goes something like this. . . . It was midmorning. The businessman was crossing town in his brand-new Jaguar. He had planned well and worked hard to get to this stage in his life. The Jaguar was not only part of his original plan but his reward for a job well done.

He needed to get to an important meeting but was reluctant to put his flawless new car at the mercy of the cabdrivers and confused out-of-towners who crowded the main thoroughfares. That's why he decided to keep to the back streets. He knew that he'd hit more stop signs this way, but he left early enough to make it to his appointment with time to spare. The route he was following took him through a tough section of town. But the streets were fairly deserted, and he wasn't planning to hesitate long enough for anyone to take a liking to his new ride.

The brick came from between two parked cars. He felt it hit somewhere on the passenger side of his Jag. He turned quickly and caught the determined look on the face of the little boy who threw it.

He practically stood on his brakes. Jumping out of his car, he raced around to the side to see the extent of the damage. The scrape was about four inches long. The impression was about one inch deep. And the gouge was about two inches wide. His blood came to an immediate boil.

The young boy was still standing between the cars where he had thrown the brick. The brick lay just a little past him on the street. The driver could see the top of his head just below the trunk line of the car closest to him. A few quick steps, and the young businessman found himself face-to-face with his assailant. Anger faced panic. Success confronted despair. A man of the world took on a little boy of the streets.

"Why did you throw that brick at my car? Do you see what you've done? Have you lost your mind?"

The boy was eight, maybe nine years old. His clothes were musty, and his body was covered with a light dusting of big-city dirt. He was visibly trembling as he looked at the angry driver. A wail burst from somewhere deep inside him, and his tears betrayed his overwhelming fear.

"Sir! Please, I'm sorry! But I was pushing my brother down the street here in his wheelchair. He's paralyzed. I'm taking him over to our grandmother's apartment. I hit a crack in the sidewalk, and his wheelchair fell over. He's on the hot sidewalk, and I can't lift him—he's too heavy. I screamed for help, but no one could hear me. I saw your car, and the only way I thought I could get your attention was to throw something at it. Please! We need your help."

The young man stared at the boy for a second and then walked past him to the sidewalk. About four cars down from where they stood, he saw the brother collapsed on his side. He raced to the boy, with the brother on his heels. The poor paraplegic was lying still with his face resting on the hot sidewalk. A puddle of tears was evaporating on the pavement beneath his head. The man immediately righted the wheelchair, pushed on its brakes, and then carefully scooped up the boy and set him in his chair. He did a swift examination of his face. It was red but not blistered from the hot concrete. His thick clothing had spared him any burns to the rest of his body.

His brick-throwing brother slipped behind the wheelchair, released the brakes, and started pushing his brother away from the businessman.

"Thanks, mister. We can make it from here. I'm sorry about your car."

The young entrepreneur watched until the two brothers made a right turn at the end of the block and disappeared around the corner, and then he walked back to study the damage to his car. The scar was ugly, dark, and deep. It drew all the attention away from his beautiful car. But it could be fixed. A few hundred dollars and the magic of a good body shop, and no one would know the difference.

But then the bigger point of what had just happened hit him with a force far greater than the brick that had damaged his car. He stared at the wound in his door for a long time. Then he looked down to the corner where he last saw the two brothers. And then he looked up . . . way up . . . up beyond the sky to the God he knew was watching. And then he shook his head in agreement.

He got in his car and drove on to his appointment. But he decided to leave the damage to his Jaguar . . . as a permanent reminder. He thought, *I want that damage to remind me to pay attention to the people and needs around me. If I'm so preoccupied*

with my own selfish goals that the only way God can get my atten-
tion is to throw a brick at me, then I'm too into myself.

There's nothing wrong with business and financial goals. There's nothing wrong with brand-new Jaguars. And there's nothing wrong with holding an enviable position on the corporate ladder. But there are two paths you can take to achieve these goals. One is preoccupied with success. The other follows the long and winding road to true greatness.

At first glance it doesn't appear to add up, but the bottom line is more than we can ever imagine when it finds its source in God's kingdom economy. One path is about what it can get. The other is about what it can give.

Let's just hope that God doesn't have to throw a brick at us to get us to choose the right one.

Ten Ways to Be a Great Teammate (For Your Kids)

1. Show up for practice on time, with a good attitude, and ready to work hard.
2. Decide at the outset that you love (not just tolerate, but love) every member of your team (athletes, coaches, trainers, and assistants).
3. Never shortcut or minimize warm-ups, calisthenics, wind sprints, distant runs, and cooldowns. These are more than just conditioning. They are part of building cohesiveness and endurance.
4. Never whine or complain about the work. It's sports; it's supposed to be difficult.
5. Don't get fixated on winning. Focus on doing the fundamentals of your position well in harmony with your fellow team members around you.
6. Listen to your body. Respond properly when it's warning you about injury (make ice, braces, tape, and Ace bandages your friends). Communicate clearly with your trainer.
7. Don't limit your involvement with team members to practice and competition. Think as a team at all times. Include

fellow teammates in your social life, family life, and academics.

8. Encourage the kids who aren't as athletic or who have extenuating circumstances that might be distracting them (problems at home, academic problems, injuries).

9. Never speak poorly of a fellow teammate or criticize the coaches. If you have a problem with a teammate or a coach, deal with that person individually.

10. When you win, win humbly. When you lose, hold your head up and never take it out on the coach or a teammate.

Bonus: Pray for your fellow teammates. Ask God to use you to bring out the best in them.

chapter five

RELEASE THE SECRET WEAPON

In the process of aiming your children at greatness, don't be surprised if you find yourself second-guessing your decision. When our firstborn child, Karis, started kindergarten, we explained to her that part of her responsibility in going to school was being a good friend to her fellow students. We encouraged her to especially reach out to kids who either didn't have friends or found it difficult to make them.

One little girl in her class was having an unusual amount of trouble connecting to the other kids. All you had to do was spend a few minutes in her home, and you knew why. Her family was hip-deep in discord. Mom and Dad were processing some serious differences in their marriage. Her siblings lacked direction. Dad was preoccupied with the front side of his career. Mom was preoccupied with bringing in enough extra money to make ends meet. These and other factors left this little girl adrift as she took her first steps into the public school system.

At this stage in a little girl's life, a mother is supposed to be helping her daughter fix her hair and pick out pretty outfits.

This is a time when a little girl needs a dad's lap to climb up on each night as she tries to unscramble the mysteries she encounters on a daily basis. This girl had very little of this kind of involvement from her parents. Often she came to school with her hair unkempt and in mismatched outfits. Her social skills were undeveloped, because that would have required her parents to be involved in grooming her for good relationships.

So, naturally, this little girl found herself on the outside looking in when it came to the relational dynamics of her classroom. She was one of the first friends our daughter made. Karis would eat lunch with her, play at recess with her, and stick close to her when the class moved as a group throughout the school. At the same time, our daughter also connected easily with all of the other kids in class.

But after a few months of school, the lines between groupings of kids were drawn as social calendars filled up with birthday parties, sleepovers, and extracurricular events. By the time our daughter entered the first grade, it was clear who the popular kids were and who they would most likely be all the way through the twelfth grade. The little girl from the distressed home wasn't on the list.

Had we put Karis on the widely accepted path to success, her relationship with this girl would have been short-lived—especially if we were emphasizing some of the priorities that parents preoccupied with the spiritual *protection* of their children often lean on. But that would have been aiming our daughter far short of the kind of target God would prefer her to hit with her life. It also would have deprived her of the challenges that forced her to rely on God's strength to get her through.

Being a friend to this girl exposed Karis to words that

weren't part of our family's vocabulary. Also, there were no adults manning the remote controls in this girl's home. Karis's friend had seen and heard a lifetime of violent and sexual scenarios by the time she was in third grade. And because no one was tutoring her on how to treat friends, she was occasionally possessive and jealous toward Karis.

The success illusion, with its worship of fame, power, beauty, and wealth, would have dictated that Karis gravitate to the kids in her class who were most likely to be assets to her personal achievement. But that would have left this girl from the troubled home with no one to be her friend.

At the time, it seemed like a lot to put on the shoulders of a six-year-old. Darcy and I had to comfort and counsel Karis through some difficult moments that occurred as a result of this friendship. We occasionally had to help her filter some morally antagonistic ideas and information.

But the biggest price of her trying to live out a pattern of greatness came from what she had to endure in the larger context of her class. This friendship cost her ridicule and rejection from the popular movers and shakers of her peer group. They'd want Karis to play with them at recess. She'd bring this girl with her. The option to play would evaporate. She'd get invited to birthday parties or sleepovers. She'd ask if they could also invite this classmate. The answer was more often in the negative than the positive. There were times when neither was invited, because they were seen as a team.

Karis even took grief from some of her friends from Sunday school because of the struggles that this girl's family was going through. We reminded her that in spite of this, she should not choose bitterness or retribution. Instead, she should just keep being a friend to everyone. In time, we believed this attitude would serve God's glory far more than the petty conflicts that often come out of being rejected.

Karis invited this girl to go to vacation Bible school with her in the summer between her third and fourth grades. The girl had a wonderful time. But things were going from bad to rotten at the friend's home, and by Christmas of that year, her parents were divorced. The little girl with the mismatched clothing and unkempt hair moved to another state a few months later. Karis assumed that she'd never see her again.

Add about fifteen years to the calendar, and out of the blue their paths once again converged. But by this time, they were both married and moms of small children. Karis's former friend had moved back to her stomping ground. She was now a beautiful young woman and conscientious wife and mother wanting to do the right thing for her new family. This girl and her husband were feeling that something was missing in their lives and decided to start going to church. The only church she knew about was the one that her former school friend, Karis, had taken her to. That is how she ended up running into Karis, and they picked up their friendship where it had left off.

God has interesting ways of bringing things full circle. Being married and a mom, this girl had started to think about spiritual things. She decided that she wanted to find out more about Jesus, the Bible, and God's plan for the human race. Karis told her about a special set of classes our church sponsored that answered those very questions. She even volunteered to attend the classes with her. The girl called her several times in the week before the classes began to talk with Karis about spiritual issues. Each time, she asked if she should bring her Bible with her to the classes. Karis thought it would help her enjoy the class much more if she did.

The girl had had this Bible since she was in elementary school. She had never read it. She had packed it many times in the numerous moves she had made, and she even considered throwing it out. But as she told Karis later, she was always afraid to throw it away "for fear God would resign me to hell!"

What neither of them remembered was how this girl got this Bible. It had been baked shut over the years of storage and nonuse. During the class, as they were sitting side by side, the girl worked the pages apart to try to find the various Scriptures that were being referenced. Karis helped her locate the verses. In the process, the Bible fell open to the front page. There, in the childish scribble of a ten-year-old, was this girl's name. Below it was this attribution: "Given on the occasion of you hiding God's Word in your heart—Karis."

Karis hadn't remembered giving it to her, but the girl recalled that it was a going-away gift when she moved after her mother's divorce. And now, after all these years, the seeds of greatness that had been planted so many years ago were coming to full bloom.

The High Cost of True Greatness

If you are going to raise kids for true greatness, it most likely will cost them some ridicule. That's because true greatness often runs against the grain of popularity, convenience, and conventional wisdom. It's risky too. Grooming kids for greatness means they might have to make their lives vulnerable to people and situations that play fast and loose with their hearts. Obviously, God has called us to a level of shrewdness when raising our kids. We need to make sure that we're monitoring what they are facing and helping them process it through the proper spiritual filters. I'm not advocating that you recklessly throw your kids to the mercy of a hostile world.

But that's why God invented righteous, godly parenting. We can create those filters in the safe harbor of our home, thereby empowering our kids to live on the front lines of their peer group and make a difference. God has not called us to raise safe kids; He's called us to raise strong ones. He hasn't called us to raise popular kids; He's called us to raise spiritually potent ones.

> God has not called us to raise safe kids; He's called us to raise strong ones.

When should the process of raising kids for greatness begin? Immediately—as soon as they can reason and take any action of their own volition. How much of their lives should they involve in the process? Every last bit of them. Every nook and cranny of their beings should be dedicated to living their lives with the qualities of true greatness.

If you spend the first eighteen years of your children's lives building this extraordinary calling into their hearts, there is no stopping the eternal impact they will have.

LET'S REVIEW OUR DEFINITION OF TRUE GREATNESS:

True greatness is a passionate love for God that demonstrates itself in an unquenchable love and concern for others.

Definitions That Lead to Profound Results

Just as sophisticated software in a computer requires a certain operating system in order to run, I'm assuming a certain spiritual operating system in you, the reader, when it comes to our discussion on true greatness.

First, I'm assuming that you know God personally, that you've made a decision to place your eternal destiny in the hands of Jesus. I'm assuming you've done that because of what He did for you by paying the price for your sins on the cross. Faith in Christ's work on Calvary is one of the prerequisites to raising kids to fulfill the definition of greatness I've given in this book.

Second, I'm assuming that you love God because of what He did for you. As your love for Him has grown, it has turned to a passionate love—a love that isn't ashamed of Him and longs to know Him more and more.

> Grace is the phenomenal power behind true greatness.

Third, I'm assuming that as a result of your love for God, you want to please Him by how you live your life and raise your kids. Obviously, we all fall short of our desires. But taking into account the normal human struggles of conscientious followers of Jesus, you still know Him, love Him, and want to live for His glory.

All that said, I want to share with you the secret weapon that fuels a heart of true greatness.

Brace yourself.

It's *grace*.

The very thing that drew us to the heart of God and keeps

us there is the very thing that God wants us to instill into our children. Grace is the phenomenal power behind true greatness. It motivates us to stand when everything else is encouraging us to run. It challenges us to reach out and engage when selfish logic says we should focus on our own best interests. It enables us to endure a lifetime of being inconvenienced on behalf of God's glory.

Grace is not just a power; it's the filter that we look through, feel through, and reason through. It makes it easy for us to behave in an illogical manner simply because grace is by its very nature illogical.

Think about it. Why would a holy, righteous God give a second thought about created beings who have worked overtime to reject everything about Him? He's given us all that we need to enjoy a fabulous and eternal love affair with Him, and instead we spurn His love, mock His law, and reject His lead in our lives. We deserve nothing less than God's complete and unbridled judgment.

But counter to the world's self-centered logic, God chooses to deal with us not according to our sin but according to His unconditional love. His holiness required that our sin be punished at the price of our physical death and our eternal separation from Him. His unconditional love stepped to the forefront of this dilemma and chose to pay that price with His own life on our behalf. Jesus's amazing grace poured from His hands, feet, and side on the cross so that we could be set free from our debt to Him. It is that grace that He now wants us to turn into action toward others.

Instilling grace into our kids is primarily going to be done by our example. But there are specific qualities of grace that we can transfer to them through formal training. I'm going to list them for you, but before I do, let's pause to remember why grace makes the most sense when it comes to formatting our children's lives. It's because grace makes it possible for us to live extraordinary and exemplary lives in spite of ourselves.

The apostle Paul was called to challenges that consistently exceeded his human capabilities, yet he rose to meet them with a power that came from the transformation he experienced through his faith in Christ. You can read his résumé for yourself in 2 Corinthians 11:21–12:10. He nails the source of that power when he puts a bottom line to his résumé. He pleaded with God to take away an inadequacy that kept him from serving Him as effectively as he could. Each time, God said, "No!" Then, finally, God told him why it wasn't necessary to remove his human inadequacies from the equation. In 2 Corinthians 12:9, He said, "My grace is enough for you. When you are weak, my power is made perfect in you" (NCV).

In the same way, God wants us to live our lives and equip our children's lives with the sheer power of His grace. When we have allowed God's grace to permeate our hearts, it's impossible to contain its impact. Two things happen: our attitudes change and our actions follow suit. And the way these altered attitudes and actions make their presence known in our lives is through an unquenchable love and concern for people.

Grace-Based Greatness

Grace-based greatness. It's a mouthful, isn't it? But it's all you need to make an indelible mark for good on history. Grace-based greatness turns you and your family into the best that you can be and makes it possible for you to bring out the best in the people who cross your path. And should you encounter some who are antagonistic to the grace that pours from your heart, so what? God's Word doesn't return void, and His grace is never a wasted effort. That's because grace runs two directions: out of us toward others, as well as back to us in joy and contentment.[1]

Here's how the matrix of true greatness looks. Grace shows itself in two attitudes, which lead to two actions. I think you're going to really like the four components that make up the matrix. Why? Because when you have them, you enjoy life more, your kids enjoy you more, and God uses all of you far more effectively.

If I were writing it out like a formula, it would look something like this:

True greatness—<u>grace</u> that demonstrates itself in the attitudes of <u>humility</u> and <u>gratefulness</u> that ultimately lead to the actions of <u>generosity</u> and a <u>servant attitude</u>

Humility, gratefulness, generosity, and a servant attitude. These are the unstoppable forces that serve our unquenchable love and concern for others. Let me build a case for this from the Bible.

Humility

What does the Bible say about humility?

- "In the same way, younger people should be willing to be under older people. And all of you should be very humble with each other. 'God is against the proud, but he gives grace to the humble'" (1 Peter 5:5–6 NCV).

○ "The LORD has told you, human, what is good; he has told you what he wants from you: to do what is right to other people, love being kind to others, and live humbly, obeying your God" (Micah 6:8 NCV).

○ "Respect for the LORD will teach you wisdom. If you want to be honored, you must be humble" (Proverbs 15:33 NCV).

What does humility look like in our children's daily lives?

○ They don't play to the crowd (or the camera) when they score the winning run or plunge over the goal line for the decisive touchdown.

○ They don't have to be first in line, insist on their way, or automatically be in charge—regardless of their leadership capabilities.

○ They don't brag about their possessions or the privileges that accompany their parents' wealth.

○ They graciously accept a compliment without a self-effacing comeback.

○ They accept victory modestly and lose with their heads held high.

Gratefulness

What does the Bible say about gratefulness?

○ "Every good action and every perfect gift is from God. These good gifts come down from the Creator of the sun, moon, and stars, who does not change like their shifting shadows. God decided to give us life through the word of truth so we might be the most important of all the things he made" (James 1:17–18 NCV).

○ "I have learned to be satisfied with the things I have and with everything that happens. I know how to live when I am poor, and I know how to live when I have plenty. I have learned the secret of being happy at any time in everything that happens, when I have enough to eat and when I go hungry, when I have more than I need and when I do not have enough. I can do all things through Christ, because he gives me strength" (Philippians 4:11–13 NCV).

What does gratefulness look like in our children's daily lives?

○ They don't whine about what they don't have or complain about what they do have.
○ They take good care of what has been provided for them.
○ They verbally express their appreciation to the people who sacrifice to help them (teachers, coaches, food servers, Sunday school teachers, youth workers, and so on).
○ They view each day with a joyful attitude regardless of the setbacks that might come their way.
○ They focus on the good things in their lives and the good qualities in the people they encounter.

Generosity

What does the Bible say about generosity?

○ "Give, and you will receive. You will be given much. Pressed down, shaken together, and running over, it

will spill into your lap. The way you give to others is
the way God will give to you" (Luke 6:38 NCV).

○ "Love . . . is not selfish" (1 Corinthians 13:4–5 NCV).

○ "God has chosen you and made you his holy people.
He loves you. So always do these things: Show mercy
to others, be kind, humble, gentle, and patient. Get
along with each other, and forgive each other. If someone does wrong to you, forgive that person because the
Lord forgave you. Do all these things; but most
important, love each other. Love is what holds you all
together in perfect unity" (Colossians 3:12–14 NCV).

What does generosity look like in our children's daily lives?

○ They view everything they have as belonging to God.

○ They set aside a portion of their allowance, gifts, or
income to give back to God and to invest in others.

○ It's second nature for them to offer the biggest piece
of pie or the last cookie to someone else.

○ They gladly surrender their rooms or their stuff when
somebody needs it more.

○ They look for ways to make someone happy with
what they have to offer (toys, clothes, food, friendship, skills, talents, and so on).

A Servant Attitude

Of the four characteristics of grace being lived out loud, this
one—serving others—is without doubt the key to making all of
the others happen. A servant attitude assumes humility, gratefulness, and generosity. Bottom line: people who don't live with

an attitude of constantly being available to serve the needs of others can never have the words "truly great" describe them—"successful," "nice," "interesting," maybe—but "truly great"—never! The one thing that unhappy families have in common is how little effort they expend investing their time in others. My friends, if you want to be happy and influence your children to greatness, serving other people needs to be an attitude that summarizes your life. Anything less, and transferring true greatness to their hearts becomes nearly impossible. With that said, let's look at this wonderful quality.

What does the Bible have to say about a servant attitude?
- "When you do things, do not let selfishness or pride be your guide. Instead, be humble and give more honor to others than to yourselves. Do not be interested only in your own life, but be interested in the lives of others" (Philippians 2:3–4 NCV).
- "So during the meal Jesus stood up and took off his outer clothing. Taking a towel, he wrapped it around his waist. Then he poured water into a bowl and began to wash the followers' feet. . . . When he had finished washing their feet, he put on his clothes and sat down again. He asked, 'Do you understand what I have just done for you? You call me "Teacher" and "Lord," and you are right, because that is what I am. If I, your Lord and Teacher, have washed your feet, you also should wash each other's feet. I did this as an example so that you should do as I have done for you. I tell you the truth, a servant is not greater than his master. A messenger is not greater than the one who

sent him. If you know these things, you will be happy
if you do them" (John 13:4–5, 12–17 NCV).

○ "Then the good people will answer, 'Lord, when did
we see you hungry and give you food, or thirsty and
give you something to drink? When did we see you
alone and away from home and invite you into our
house? When did we see you without clothes and give
you something to wear? When did we see you sick or
in prison and care for you?' Then the King will
answer, 'I tell you the truth, anything you did for even
the least of my people here, you also did for me'"
(Matthew 25:37–40 NCV).

What does a servant attitude look like in our children's daily lives?

○ They don't grumble or complain when they are asked
to do their chores.

○ They look for ways to help people who need a hand
up in life.

○ They realize that serving others isn't always personally
appreciated or publicly recognized, and they don't take
it personally.

○ Before they leave a gathering, they do everything they
can to help the host put everything back in order
(equipment stored away after a sporting event, toys
put away in the nursery or Sunday school class, dishes
washed and furniture put back in place after a party,
and so on).

○ Instead of expecting to be waited on at home, they
assume responsibility for themselves and offer to help
their parents and siblings.

When we instill these profound qualities into our children, we set them up to live a life that makes an eternal difference. And if our children happen to gain a portion of fame, power, beauty, and wealth along the way, these things will merely supplement their ability to live for true greatness.

But to see this happen in our children's lives, we must become the gold standard of greatness through our own example. Our children need to see us model a consistent servant attitude in life.

THE GOLD STANDARD OF GREATNESS

Our children need to see parents who are absolutely sold out to God and serving Him passionately. They need to see this . . .

. . . in our overall attitude toward life.

. . . in our view toward others.

. . . in our view toward our possessions.

. . . in our view toward the less fortunate.

. . . in our response to the church.

. . . in our view toward our spouse.

. . . in our view toward our children.

. . . in our response to suffering and hardship.

. . . in our response to temptation.

. . . in our commitment to absolute integrity.

. . . in our attitude toward life's inconveniences.

. . . in our attitude toward God's Word and prayer.

. . . in our relationship with God.

Presuppositions That Lead to True Greatness

God's grace is the most effective weapon when it comes to combating loneliness, despair, arrogance, ignorance, elitism, racism, bigotry, isolation, poverty, and unresolved anger. When we release this secret weapon, hell doesn't break loose; it runs for cover.

God's grace, working in us and through us as parents, creates power and filters that enable us to aim for greatness. As we model this grace to our children, it energizes them when they're asked to do difficult or sacrificial things like befriend the hard to love or use their money to buy Bibles for people who may not read them for decades.

Grace changes our presuppositions toward everything we have and toward every person who crosses our path. In fact, it turns us into one of the most attractive types of thinkers anyone could want to be. It's called an "abundant thinker." This kind of thinking is foundational to our ability to accurately choose our mission, our mates, and our master in life.

In the next chapter, we're going to find out what abundant thinkers look like up close and personal.

Ten Ways to Be a Great Classmate (For Your Kids)

1. Be a friend to everyone in your class, not just the popular kids.
2. Invite the kids who are consistently left out of activities to play with you or walk with you between classes, especially the poor kids or kids who represent a racial minority in your school. Never let anyone eat alone at lunch (especially the geeks). Invite them to eat with you. If you are part of the popular crowd, insist on these other kids being a part of it too. If the popular kids reject you in the process, so be it.
3. Be pleasant to everyone, especially your teacher. Smile, look people in the eyes, call them by name, and be interested in them as individuals.
4. Don't allow yourself to be drawn into antagonism against your teacher—whether in the classroom or elsewhere. Refuse the peer pressure to be disruptive, regardless of whether your teacher is asking for it.
5. Never allow yourself to be drawn into a group conspiracy against your teacher. Whether it's fellow students or their parents, deal with any problem you have with your

teacher individually. Avoid any attempt by the class or their parents to gang up on a teacher regarding an issue.

6. Help students who may be struggling to connect to the class or figure out the subject. As much as possible, do whatever you can to raise the emotional and intellectual stock value of the entire classroom.

7. Don't hog discussions, show off your intellect, or critique fellow students' answers in such a way as to embarrass them.

8. When you go to bed at night, pray for your teacher and fellow students who may be struggling.

9. Be an enthusiastic participant in the greater school activities. Cheer on and encourage your teams, applaud the kids who gain recognition for their great efforts, and always speak well of your school.

10. Recognize that there are some kids around you who are either extremely afraid or are having to process some heavy burden (problems at home, the divorce of the parents, a mom or dad who is sick, a sibling who is struggling). Ask God to give you a keen sense of who these kids are, and make it your aim to encourage them every day.

chapter six

LIVING LARGE BY THINKING BIG

There is a huge difference between people who do great things and people who live great lives. Doing great things demands that you rise to a momentary challenge and perform the requirements of that moment extremely well. Living a great life demands that you rise to the challenges you face in all areas of your life, over and over again, day after day, for a prolonged period of time. The former can earn you an honorable place in history. We often refer to these people as "heroes." The latter gives you a chance to reformat history. These are the truly great people. We need to keep this in mind as we contrast the two types of thinkers.

There is no comparison between the finite human mind and the infinite wisdom of God. That doesn't mean, however, that we are not supposed to align our thoughts with the thought processes of God. The Bible says that, as Christians, "we have the mind of Christ" (1 Corinthians 2:16 NCV).

Contradiction? Not even close. It's simply a case of perspective. Human beings will never be able to troll the depths of

God's immeasurable intellect. God is omniscient. We'll never be. But God became man for several reasons, one of which was for us to get a close look at His heart so that we could learn to think abundantly.

A good example of abundant thinking can be found in John 6. It was late in the afternoon. A large crowd had gathered around Jesus. They had been stalking Him most of the day, so He had obliged them with some phenomenal teaching about the kingdom of God. They hung on every word. Some had gotten close enough to see the amazing look of love in His eyes. A few even got to feel His healing touch.

Jesus studied the crowd and then turned to one of His disciples, Philip, and asked, "Where shall we buy bread for these people to eat?" (v. 5). The text says that He did this to test Philip, because Jesus already knew what He was going to do.

Jesus wasn't trying to make Philip look foolish in front of everyone. That's not His style. As always, He was dealing with Philip and everyone else there according to His overwhelming love. In fact, at this moment in Philip's life, Jesus was showing an amazing sense of compassion. Of course, Jesus had a practical compassion for the people who were getting hungry. But He also had a specific compassion for Philip and the other disciples.

Let me define the term: *compassion* is seeing a person's needs in advance and doing everything within your power to minimize their liabilities and maximize their potential. The immediate need was a large crowd of hungry people. But Jesus was dealing with another need. He knew that in a very short period of time, He would be leaving the earth. At His ascension into heaven, He would give His disciples the mandate to establish and care for His church (Matthew 28:19–20; Acts 1:8).

But think about it: how many people made up "the church" when Jesus gave the order to establish it? If you were counting using your fingers and toes, you'd still have a few digits left.

How much money would they have had in the bank when they were given their orders to evangelize the world?

None.

How much property would they have owned?

None.

Jesus knew that He was going to call these men to do exceptional things and follow extraordinary orders when there was absolutely no way it could be done with their own human capabilities. Yet He wanted them to follow His commands without hesitation. He wanted them to know that when they did things in His power, there was no limit to what they could do.

> Compassion is seeing a person's needs in advance and doing everything within your power to minimize their liabilities and maximize their potential.

Using the questions we raised as a springboard, let's update them.

How many people make up the living body of Christ *today*? A couple of *billion*.

How much property does the organized church hold in trust? Hundreds of thousands of acres, not counting the buildings and their contents.

What are the physical assets of the church worth today? Trillions.

In John 6:1–14, Jesus's immediate purpose was to feed a hungry crowd. But His bigger purpose was to teach the disciples a vital lesson in how to think. He was saying, in essence, "When I tell you to do something and there is no way humanly possible for you to do it, just do it! I'll empower you!" That's what caused Him to take a Happy Meal some thoughtful mother had sent with her son and multiply it enough not only to feed every person in the crowd "as much as they wanted" but also to fill an entire basket for each disciple (John 6:11). In the process, He was saying to His disciples, "I'll empower you to do the bigger-than-life things I ask you to do, and I will also take care of the needs of you and your family at the same time." It was a potent lesson that the disciples got to play an active role in learning.

Jesus used a teaching method that is often used today in our classrooms. He gave a laboratory demonstration and then followed it with a pop quiz.

When the disciples finished feeding the people and had gathered up all that remained of the fish-and-chips meal, Jesus asked them to start across the lake ahead of Him. In Matthew 14:22, He specifically said that they were to go ahead and He would meet them on the other side of the lake.

Then came *the test*.

As the disciples were making what should have been a fairly brief voyage across the lake, a violent storm dropped down on top of them. Hours after they should have been on shore, they were still in the middle of the lake, buffeted by the choppy waves and blown sideways by the wind. They were straining at the oars and rowing for their lives when Jesus came walking past the boat on the surface of the water. I'm willing to admit that, had I been part of the crew, I probably would have responded the same way they did.

"A ghost!" they screamed, at which point Jesus gave them the number one piece of advice He gave to people throughout His public ministry: "Don't be afraid" (Mark 6:50). The account in Mark goes on to say, "Then he climbed into the boat with them, and the wind died down. They were completely amazed, for they had not understood about the loaves; their hearts were hardened" (vv. 51–52).

What didn't the disciples understand about the miracle of feeding the five thousand? Answer: Everything! Jesus was trying to tell them that when it came to doing His work, *think abundantly*. A little bit of nothing, in the hands of ordinary people, can accomplish extraordinary things through the power of God.

Here the disciples were, frightened out of their minds, wondering if they were going to make it through the storm alive. But what was the last thing Jesus had said to them? He had said to go ahead of Him across the lake and He would meet them *on the other side*. The other side—as in the shoreline . . . dry land . . . safety. For the disciples to entertain even the smallest thought about perishing was to get an F on their quiz. It was absolutely *impossible* for them to drown—even if their boat sank.

I like the way John's account concludes the story: "Then they were willing to take him into the boat, and *immediately* the boat reached the shore where they were heading" (John 6:21, emphasis added).

Immediately. On the shore. Right where He said He would meet them.

True Greatness and Abundant Thinking

There is an inseparable connection between raising kids for greatness and thinking abundantly. These are more than kissing cousins; they are conjoined twins.

As we have seen, true greatness is a passionate love for God that shows itself in an unquenchable love and concern for people. It is based in grace. Its attitudes are humility and gratefulness. Its actions are generosity and a servant attitude.

Overriding the entire formula is a commitment to abundant thinking. It's living large by thinking big. Parents who embody God's spirit of abundance in the way they treat each other, their kids, and everyone they encounter create one of the best environments for preparing kids for greatness in every dimension of their adult lives.

Great people lead great lives in the midst of all the inequities and disparities that trip up everybody else. It's not just the age-old perspective of viewing the glass half-full as opposed to half-empty. Abundant thinkers are realistic; they can see when the waterline of the glass is getting low. But that honest appraisal doesn't dictate their overall attitude. Their moods are not at the mercy of their circumstances.

> There is an inseparable connection between raising kids for greatness and thinking abundantly.

People who think abundantly are enjoyable to be around, fun to work with, and usually easier to look at, regardless of their physical attributes. Because fear doesn't hold them in its grip and they view anxiety as something to master rather than something to be mastered by, they tend to show a lot less age on their faces. They're happy, positive people who maintain a generous attitude toward life. Kids who grow up around mothers and fathers who smile a lot, cheer a lot, sing a lot, dance a lot, dream a lot, and laugh a lot find it much easier to embrace a similar attitude when they become adults.

Scarcity Thinking

There is an opposite attitude that is far more pervasive and is no respecter of persons. It permeates the thinking patterns of men or women, old or young, educated or uneducated, Christian or otherwise. It's sad to see this attitude coming from Christians, since it is an absolute contradiction of the heart and character of God; but it exists nonetheless. In fact, I'd say it dominates the mainstream thinking of rank-and-file Christians. I like to refer to this mind-set as "scarcity thinking."

It's everywhere. You hear it when people talk, you sense it in the way they pray, and you see it in how they view the people close to them. It shows in how they appraise strangers, how they manage their time, and how they view their possessions.

And it is toxic beyond belief. A home characterized by scarcity thinking is one of the most debilitating environments anyone could live in. It limits love, it blunts potential, and it robs people of hope. Scarcity thinkers steal joy and pollute grace. And here's the kicker: scarcity thinkers are usually the last ones to see their problem. They bring out the worst in the folks around them, but they seldom figure out that they're the ones standing on everyone's air hose.

In this chapter, I will contrast these two basic ways of thinking. I'll compare them as they process a handful of primary questions that all people must ask as they go through their day-to-day lives. As we look at these two attitudes, I urge you to be honest as you appraise yourself in light of what you are reading.

Our Presuppositions Affect Our Conclusions

Presuppositions. We all have them. These are the starting points of our thinking patterns and are at the core of our most fundamental beliefs. In fact, they are the most accurate assessors of what we truly believe. They also determine our thinking process and the conclusions we ultimately come to. They are like road markers that we use to get from point A to point B in our minds.

Here's the problem: if our presuppositions are wrong, our thinking will be flawed and our conclusions inaccurate. Because none of us is an island, the conclusions we come to affect the people who surround us. More important, the way we think and the conclusions we come to have the power to imprint themselves on the malleable value system of our children. If we're flawed, we have the power to send them into adulthood handicapped in their own thinking. That's why it is essential for us to accurately assess our presuppositions.

One more thing: our presuppositions correlate directly with the amount of love we have for God and the amount of confidence we have in His Word. The deeper our love and the greater the confidence we place in His Word, the more reliable our presuppositions will be. The more reliable our presuppositions are, the more accurate our thinking will be. The more accurate our thinking is, the more dependable and workable our conclusions will be. Sound conclusions create good choices . . . one right after another. This turns us into people of value—people who live great lives.

With these thoughts in the back of our minds, let's run these two types of thinkers through some basic filters.

How Do They View Life?

Scarcity Thinkers

Scarcity thinkers start with the presupposition that life is finite. They assume that everything is limited. This affects 100 percent of their attitudes. Here are some basic things that they assume have lids on them:

- Ideas . . . limited.
- Resources . . . limited.
- Imagination . . . limited.
- Opportunities . . . limited.
- Love . . . limited.

These kinds of thinkers are no fun to go on vacation with. They are miserable to deal with when you are facing a crisis. They are wet blankets in boardrooms. They can wreck a company that happens to be on a roll. They are hard to wake up next to. Most of all, they have a way of taking the wind out of your sails if they happen to be your parents. They automatically bring out the worst in the people who are close to them.

When you assume that life is finite, you automatically

focus on yourself. Life becomes one grand conspiracy. Scarcity thinkers are insecure, feel insignificant, and struggle with an overwhelming sense of personal inadequacy. This causes them to overcompensate by filling these voids in their lives with material things, money, applause, recognition, abuse, power, and high control.

Because scarcity thinking is so debilitating, scarcity thinkers have a hard time finding good work or staying employed. The liabilities that permeate their attitude make it clear to the people who are doing the hiring that this person would be an overall drain on the company. If they own a company, they have a hard time getting good people to work for them for a prolonged period of time. Scarcity thinkers have a difficult time staying married. Their negative view of life makes the reasons obvious. They also often create tension in their homes and incite far more rivalry among siblings than is normal or necessary. Scarcity thinkers breed the mindset, "Everyone for themselves!" Children figure, "I'd better fight for my position in this family, because if I don't, I'll lose what little I already have."

Abundant Thinkers

Abundant thinkers, on the other hand, start with the presupposition that all the good things in life have no boundaries. When it comes to what life has to offer, they assume that there is plenty for everyone. This permeates 100 percent of their attitude. This causes them to look at the same list that scarcity thinkers look at with completely opposite assumptions:

- ○ Ideas . . . unlimited.
- ○ Resources . . . unlimited.

○ Imagination . . . unlimited.
○ Opportunities . . . unlimited.
○ Love . . . unlimited.

These kinds of thinkers are a blast to go on vacation with. They are exactly who you want in your life when you are facing a crisis. They are coolheaded under pressure, deliberate, and balanced. They are exciting in boardrooms. They can take a company on a roll and increase the speed of its success exponentially. They are a lot of fun to wake up next to. Most of all, they have a way of filling a child's sails with the kind of motivating wind that can get them to the deeper waters of adulthood safely. Abundant thinkers bring out the best in the people up close to them.

When you assume that all the good things in life are unlimited, you automatically focus outward. Life becomes one grand opportunity to make a positive difference. Abundant thinkers feel secure, significant, and strong in the Lord. Because they've found the true source of these needs through their relationships with God, they take on adulthood emotionally healthy, empowered by God to make an amazing difference.

Abundant thinkers are driven to greatness by their desire to love people, carry out a great purpose, and transfer hope to as many people as they can. This gives them balance when it comes to money and material things, praise and recognition, and the exercise of influence. Kids who live with these kinds of parents relax and enjoy their childhood. Abundant thinking enables them to build their internal lives carefully and well.

Abundant thinkers find it easier to attain work and stay employed. Their attitude makes it clear to the people who are doing the hiring that they would be an overall boost to the company team. If they own a company, they have an easier time getting good people to work for them and stick with them. Abundant thinkers find it easier to stay married because they are so much easier to live with. Their positive view of life makes the reasons obvious. Their kids are more inclined to obey them and cooperate with them. They create an esprit de corps that breeds a natural harmony between siblings. Kids tend to treat each other the way they are treated. When Dad and Mom assume there are plenty of all the good things in life for everyone, the kids find it easy to pick up this same theme toward each other. They are more complimentary, helpful, and empathetic with their siblings.

Abundant thinking finds its source in an abundant God. Jesus said, "The thief does not come except to steal, and to kill, and to destroy. I have come that they may have life, and that they may have it more abundantly" (John 10:10 NKJV). Abundant thinkers encourage their children's dreams, undergird their hopes, and maximize their potential. It's simply the logical outgrowth of trusting in a God who cannot be contained.

Abundant thinkers assume the following:

○ The best ideas haven't been thought up yet.
○ The best books have yet to be written.
○ The best companies have yet to be incorporated.
○ The best songs have yet to be sung.
○ The best sermons haven't been preached yet.
○ The best years of their marriage are still ahead.
○ The best memories of their family are waiting to be made.

It's all based on the presuppositions you start out with when it comes to your overall view of life. Where you finish has everything to do with where you start.

Keep in mind that you can be a Christian and also be a scarcity thinker; you will just find it more difficult to raise kids for greatness.

How Do They View What They Have?

Scarcity Thinkers

Scarcity thinkers have a hard time sharing. They hoard. Remember, for them, life is finite. So . . . what do they hoard?

- They hoard recognition.
- They hoard ideas.
- They hoard opportunities.
- They hoard power.
- They hoard their time.
- They hoard profit.
- They hoard resources.
- They hoard love.

Not only do they do this for themselves, but their small view of life causes them to hoard their children's lives. Scarcity thinkers are known for orchestrating the best-case scenario for their children even at the expense of fairness to others. Because they fear not getting a big enough piece of the pie, they are not above encouraging their children to withhold information, take short-cuts, and even cheat if it gets them a bigger share. I've watched scarcity-thinking parents want victory so badly for their children that they even tutor them to do harm if it gets the desired result. Be it injury in sports or misrepresentation of facts in academics, whatever it takes to destroy the competition is fair game if it increases their child's chances of success.

Every time I see parents instilling this selfish mind-set into their children, I always think the same thing: *Get ready, Mom. Brace yourself, Dad. Those awful skills you are teaching your child are ultimately going to be used against you.*

Scarcity thinkers treat what they have the same way they treat people; they tend to be cheap. Most are lousy tippers.

Abundant Thinkers

Abundant thinkers hold all that they have in an open palm. It's not that they are irresponsible with what God has given them. In fact, they are careful stewards of their personal assets and intellectual property. But they want to use all of these things to better everyone around them. They get great joy out of using all that they have to bring the best out of as many people as they can. It's simply the logical extension of the mind of Christ.

Abundant thinkers *share*. So . . . what do they share?

- They share recognition.
- They share ideas.
- They share opportunities.
- They share power.
- They share their time.
- They share profit.
- They share resources.
- They share love.

Because there is plenty for everyone, abundant thinkers don't want their children getting ahead at the expense of someone who is more deserving. That's because they are not viewing their children as limited. They already see their children as winners simply because they exist. They already see them with unlimited value and potential.

And abundant-thinking parents are not afraid to let their children experience their fair share of difficulties or defeats. That's because they are far more interested in the character of their children than their accomplishments. Plus, kids growing up around abundant-thinking parents don't have to perform or make their parents look better in order to get love. Love is never hoarded by abundant thinkers; it's shared in unlimited supply.

Abundant thinkers treat what they have the same way they treat people; they are generous. They're great tippers.

How Do They View Others?

Scarcity Thinkers

Scarcity thinkers have a difficult time being genuinely happy for the successes of other people—even, and especially, members of their own family, close friends, and associates. They treat other people's successes as though something has been taken from them. It goes back to their presupposition that life is like a finite pie. Everything is limited. If someone else gets something good, the scarcity thinker assumes that there is less left for him- or herself.

Let's say a scarcity thinker opens his garage and notices his next-door neighbor cleaning the windshield of a brand-new Hummer. Let's listen in on the exchange:

Neighbor: Hey, look what I just got.

ST: A Hummer.

Neighbor: Yeah. A Hummer . . . brand-new.

ST: Things must be going well for you at work?

Neighbor: They're going all right. But I didn't buy this. My grandmother bought it for me.

ST: Your grandmother bought you a Hummer?

Neighbor: Yeah. Crazy, isn't it? You see, she's got a lot of money and figured it's all going to get taxed into oblivion if she doesn't do something with it. She's got all she needs, so she decided to start giving it out to her family members. Bought us all cars . . . and paid the taxes on them for us too. So you want to take it for a spin?

ST: No!

Neighbor: You sure? It's a lot of fun when you get behind the wheel.

ST: Nope! Too busy! Gotta go!

The scarcity thinker goes in his house fuming. He says to his wife, "Did you see what our neighbor has in his driveway? It's a brand-new Hummer. His *grandmother* bought it for him! She even paid the taxes on it. I can't stand that guy."

If his neighbor beeps the horn at him as he's going to or from work, the scarcity thinker says to himself, "Boy, I hate that car!" He comes home and sees his neighbor looking at something on the door of his Hummer:

ST: What's wrong?

Neighbor: Somebody nicked my door in the parking lot at work.

ST: (Under his breath) Yes! That thing's starting to look
more and more like the piece of junk I drive.

Pathetic, isn't it? Heartbreaking beyond words. The only
thing that's worse is if this scarcity thinker has procreated. His
poor children have to go into adulthood saddled with this sorry
attitude. What's really sad is that scarcity thinkers miss out on
all of the shared blessings because they refuse to acknowledge
another person's joy. If they can't be blessed, they don't want
anyone else to be blessed.

Scarcity thinkers take regular doses of the cultural poison pill
known as *comparison*. They compare spouses, children's accomplishments, bottom lines, and blessings. If something nice happens to someone close to them, it's not unusual for scarcity
thinkers to want to rain on their picnic.

Abundant Thinkers

Abundant thinkers, on the other hand, love it when good
things happen to others, especially family members, friends,
and associates. They can't applaud their friend's or family member's accomplishments or good fortune enough. In the process,
they get to partake in that person's joy.

Let's take the same scenario with the neighbor, but this time
it's an abundant thinker who comes out of his garage to dis-
cover his neighbor cleaning the windshield of a brand-new
Hummer:

Neighbor: Hey, look what I just got.
AT: A Hummer!
Neighbor: Yeah. A Hummer . . . brand-new.

AT: That's fantastic! Things must be going well for you at work!

Neighbor: They're going all right. But I didn't buy this. My grandmother bought it for me.

AT: Your grandmother bought you a Hummer? That's even better!

Neighbor: Yeah. Crazy, isn't it? You see, she's got a lot of money and figured it's all going to get taxed into oblivion if she doesn't do something with it. She's got all she needs, so she decided to start giving it out to her family members. Bought us all cars . . . and paid the taxes on them for us too. So you want to take it for a spin?

AT: You'll let me drive it? Cool! Just a second and let me tell my wife where I'm going.

The abundant thinker goes in his house dancing. He says to his wife, "Honey! You won't believe what our neighbor has in his driveway. It's a brand-new *Hummer*. And get this: his *grandmother* bought it for him! Even paid the taxes on it. Is that incredible? I *love* that guy. He's going to let me take it for a spin. Come with me and check it out. Bring the camera; I want to get my picture taken next to him with his new car."

If his neighbor beeps the horn at him as he's going to or from work, the abundant thinker says to himself, "Boy, I love that car!" He comes home and sees his neighbor looking at something on the door of his Hummer:

AT: What's wrong?

Neighbor: Somebody nicked my door in the parking lot at work.

AT: Oh no! . . . Wait a minute, I've got some compound
in my garage. Let me grab it and come on over. I think
we can rub that nick out!

What's the difference? It's like the neighbor's grandmother
gave the *abundant thinker* the car. He is so excited for all the
wonderful things that happen to the people around him, it's as
though they were happening to him. That's because when
abundant thinkers see someone else, they see a person with
intrinsic value.

There is no comparison to the head start that kids living in
abundant-thinking families have when it comes to growing
into adults who model true greatness. When abundant thinking is all around you when you're growing up, it comes more
naturally when it's finally your turn to lead a generation.

How Do They View Adversity?

Scarcity Thinkers

Scarcity thinkers take adversity personally and want to punish the people close to them when they have to go through it.
What are some of the standard ways scarcity thinkers react to
adversity? They whine. They complain. They nag. Someone has
well said that nagging is like being nibbled to death by a duck.
It's so *annoying*. You want to say to the person, "For Pete's sake,
why don't you just grow teeth and finish me off? This incessant
nagging is driving me nuts!"

Scarcity thinkers don't dream, and they don't give the people
close to them permission to dream. People who dream are simply setting out some hopes in the future that they can claim

later. Hebrews 11:1 says, "Faith is the substance of things hoped for, the evidence of things not seen" (NKJV). When you start out with a limited view of God and an unwillingness to put your complete confidence in His mighty love, you end up ruining the dreams of the people around you. Kids who live in scarcity-thinking homes want to grow up to experience great adult lives, just like the kids in abundant-thinking homes. Unfortunately, when it comes to achieving those great lives, they're on their own.

Abundant Thinkers

Abundant thinkers, on the other hand, feel the pain and frustration of adversity, but they don't use it as an excuse for inactivity. Instead, they do everything within their power to move beyond it. And when they are operating under the presupposition that they have all the power of God working from inside them, as Ephesians 3:20–21 says, then they have a much higher success ratio of turning adversity into an asset.

What are some of the standard ways that abundant thinkers respond to adversity? They fall forward. It's an analogy from football. They know they are going to get tackled. They know they are going to face hardship as they go through life. They know that they are going to get knocked down; they just want to gain some ground when that happens to them. Just like in football, if you keep falling forward when you get tackled, eventually you fall across the goal line and get some numbers up on the scoreboard.

Abundant thinkers don't resent the hurts that come their way. They realize that pain is a part of life. It's a part of relationships. It almost always accompanies the process of trying to do extraordinary things.

Abundant thinking comes a lot easier when you aren't playing for yourself or even for the crowd—but rather you are playing for the Coach. When all you're trying to do with each breath you take is live for God's glory, adversity doesn't get the best of you.

One thing we know about our children: they will no doubt face more than their share of adversity on their paths to greatness. It will be so much easier for them to process their pains and disappointments if they see someone modeling abundant thinking throughout their childhoods.

When life is not about you and it's all about God, it's so much easier to view your possessions, the people who surround you, and even the adversity that comes your way through the power of an abundant attitude. And when you factor in all those young people who are waking up in your home each morning just wanting a chance at true greatness, it's really the least you can do.

Ten Ways to Be a Great Friend (For Your Kids)

1. Never disparage your friends' parents. No matter how much your friends are struggling, always encourage them to do their best to love and respect their mom and dad.

2. Don't tease your friends regarding things they are sensitive about (their looks, their weight, their intellect, their family, etc.).

3. Never let them talk you into doing wrong or having fun at someone else's expense. Rise above this. You'll be a much better friend to them if you do.

4. Don't smother them, and don't let them smother you. Friends give each other plenty of space. Encourage them to spend time with their families and other friends.

5. Be trustworthy with private information they share with you. Never use their vulnerability against them.

6. Encourage them when they're down, and applaud them when they've put forth a good effort (in sports, in academics, in relationships, etc.).

7. Make it your aim to help your friends become better people in all areas of their

lives (physically, emotionally, intellectually, morally, spiritually, and in regard to their talents).

8. Be loyal and faithful to your friends should they fall out of favor with the popular crowd or happen to be struggling through a difficult time in their lives (drugs, alcohol, rebellion against their parents, rejection of academic responsibilities, etc.).

9. Be a "fun" friend to be around. Let your hair down. Don't be a "stick in the mud." Enjoy your times together.

10. Pray for your friends. Ask God to use you to build them up and help them feel better about themselves.

chapter seven

HELPING YOUR CHILDREN CHOOSE A GREAT MASTER IN LIFE

U h-oh. We have to shift gears and discuss something difficult here. Up to this point, we've enjoyed a nice, harmless jaunt through our conversation on true greatness. Wisdom says I should play it safe and maintain an "Oprah" relationship with the reader. As you know, Oprah is a wonderful lady who likes to talk about a lot of nice topics and fun human interest stories. Not to imply that Oprah confines herself to merely "safe" topics. In fact, Oprah covers some of the most provocative issues of the day with depth and passion. But Oprah is a kind and gracious woman. She wears like a comfortable sweater. Then there's Dr. Phil, who has become famous for his in-your-face bluntness and "How's that working for you?" honesty. Oprah . . . Dr. Phil . . . Oprah . . . Dr. Phil . . . hmm?

I choose Dr. Phil.

I don't think Oprah would mind, since she introduced Dr. Phil to us in the first place.

Here's the rub: the idea of being a servant doesn't sit well with the average person. And when you use the term *master* to describe the one whom you are serving, the idea loses its appeal even more. Master assumes slave. Many parents choose to dismiss this icky concept of servanthood when preparing their kids for true greatness, but this is a tragic mistake. That's because being a servant isn't an option in life; it's a foregone conclusion. Every human being is going to serve someone or something.

For most of us, it was in our literature class in high school that we were introduced to William Earnest Henley's famous rhyme "Invictus," which closes with the classic line, "I am the master of my fate; I am the captain of my soul."

No, William, you're not.

You *never* were.

Nobody is.

The only free choice we exercise in life is whose servant we are going to be. After that, the natural consequences of our choice take over. Failure to understand this not only creates a gaping hole in our plans to prepare our children for true greatness, but we actually set up our kids to be mastered by the very things that cause them to fail.

> We are not in charge of our lives.

Our children are born with a natural inclination toward accommodating their own desires. Left to themselves without any moral limitations or directions, our children would grow into self-destructive nightmares. The Bible refers to this inclination as "the cravings of sinful man, the lust of his eyes and the boasting of what he has and does" (1 John 2:16). It says, "We all, like sheep, have gone astray, each of us has turned to his own way" (Isaiah 53:6). This causes us to want to control as many things that connect to our lives as possible. We want to control the status of our possessions, our health, our relationships, and the way people view us. But we don't actually have that power; we're just led to believe that we do. In reality, we are far more at the mercy of the overarching forces that operate around us.

It's very tempting to go into a deep and layered theological study on the competition for our hearts, but the purpose of this book is to simplify the complex. On top of that, you don't need a heavily annotated theological study to convince you of what should be as obvious as the nose on your face. We are not in charge of our lives. Either the God of creation is in charge of our lives, or we're controlled by our flesh, the corrupted world system, or the devil. And to be fair to the devil (why I'd want to do that, I'm not sure), he simply uses our weak flesh and the corrupted world system that surrounds us to do his vile bidding. His goal in everything he does is to steal glory from God. Few things steal as much glory from God as an individual who was bought and paid for on a cross but has no desire to submit to the conditions of the purchase agreement. We must never forget what we cost. We cost God His Son. We cost Jesus His life. Real blood poured down the cross so that we could be redeemed from our enslavement to sin.

Every last one of us is in a state of servitude to someone or something. The only ones who get a taste of true greatness are the ones who have chosen to submit their lives to the right master. Those who choose to give their lives totally to the authority of God place themselves in the hands of One who actually has their best interests at heart. Not only that, but they put their lives in submission to the only personal power that is greater than the collective power of all of the forces of the universe combined.

Who's on First?

God is not here for us; we're here for Him. He was first. And long after we're off the scene, God will still be. That's because He *is*, whereas we simply just *are*. We didn't come up with God for our benefit; He created us for His glory.

Any parent who wants to raise children who achieve true greatness must grasp the significance of the sovereign preeminence of God. This doesn't come easy to most parents for three reasons.

The first reason is the most obvious: *we're selfish by nature.* Our flawed internal wiring would prefer that our places and positions in life get top billing, even at the expense of the Creator of the universe. The only people we might want to have a higher billing would be our children. We are motivated by our goals, our needs, our hopes, our interests, our fears, our desires, our time, our space, our opinions, our money, our agendas, our pleasures, our likes, our dislikes, our wants, our dreams, and our individual tastes. So are our children.

> God is not here for us; we're here for Him.

And then there's the second reason: *everything around us tells us to follow our desire to have our own way.* Ours is an egocentric culture that promotes the worship of self and panders to the priority of personal preferences. Part of this culture is simply the accommodation of our uniqueness. After all,

God is all about variety and originality. It makes perfect sense, therefore, that there should be myriad options available to us when it comes to the basic things of life, like how we dress ourselves, what we eat, what kind of music we listen to, what we do for a living, and so on. But our culture still serves to undergird our inclination to make ourselves the center of the universe by encouraging us to seek our own interests regardless of how it affects the people around us (or the God we serve). If our children aren't carefully tutored on how to handle this culture, they could easily assume that their present, as well as their future, is all about them.

Then there's the third reason we tend to get things backward when it comes to our attitude about God: *we think that God is supposed to be at our beck and call.* Unfortunately, this attitude is promoted at times even by our spiritual leaders. Obviously, God loves to bless His children. He cares for us, goes before us to protect us, and constantly serves as a rear guard against the things we can't possibly see coming. God is a giver of gifts. He's the sustainer of life. He is the Great Physician. Libraries cannot contain the books that catalog the extent of His love, grace, mercy, and blessing. But He's not our personal genie.

Fortunately, most reasonable students of the Bible can see the holes that riddle the health-and-wealth movement. All you have to do is spend an evening worshiping with some of the spiritual champions who live each day at street level in the inner city, and you realize that truly great faith has nothing to do with money. Watch a sweet, humble saint slip into the vise grip of Alzheimer's, and you quickly figure out that God's promised blessings in the Bible don't guarantee that you won't have to live a few years in death's waiting room.

But health-and-wealth theology is not the real trap for most Christians. Its hollow and selfish ring is too obvious. Rather, the bigger trap for us is the subtle tendency to shift our attitude from our being here for God to God's being here for us. That's because we're the ones showing up with all the needs. We are the ones who could use a little more money, better opportunities, nicer surroundings, and a few more uplifting people around us.

And we're the ones who want everything to work out best for our kids.

It's Not About You

One of the great debates in literature has to do with who penned the best opening line in a book. Charles Dickens usually gets a lot of votes for his pithy start to *A Tale of Two Cities*: "It was the best of times; it was the worst of times." When you read this powerful story of redemption and exchanged lives set against the backdrop of the French Revolution, you realize just how inspired Dickens must have felt when he inked those words.

Another powerful opening line is the one you find at the front of Rick Warren's influential work, *The Purpose-Driven Life*. Few Christian books in history have captured the true essence of our relationship to God better than this one. And the four words set by themselves on the first line of the book summarize the heart of his message.

"It's not about you."[1]

Life isn't about you or me. It's not about our children or our plans for them. It is 100 percent about God. It's *all* about God and *His* plans for us.

If life is all about God and not about you or me, then we do well to instill this truth into our children from the moment they take their first breaths. That's because between the time of their first breaths and their last, either they are going to be part of God's overarching plan for the world, or they are going to stand against it. Either way, the bigger story will never be about them. It will be about the Creator of their lives and the true Author of the amazing story that God wants to write with their lives.

And that's exactly what God wants our children's lives to be: an utterly *amazing* story—sustained with a secure love, driven by a significant purpose, and supported by a strong hope. God wants our children to grow up knowing all about His grace and understanding how His unmerited kindness has set them free. He wants them to be key players in His unfolding drama of redemption. He wants them to glorify Him and enjoy Him continually throughout every moment of their existence.

Obviously, it's hard to transfer this essential concept in a theoretical fashion. Making God the source, the first, the last, and the center of your children's lives isn't going to happen as a result of some strategic pep talks around the dinner table. The preeminence of God isn't transferred in part-time lessons or sound-bite principles. Rather, it's embodied in real-time life. Kids don't grasp this intellectually unless it is modeled for them individually.

Which brings up another great opening line of a book:

"In the beginning, God . . ."

The Bible leads off with this overriding theme. From beginning to end, the Bible is the story of God's involvement with the human race. We are the objects of his affection, but He is the star of the show. Unfortunately, it is too easy to want the spotlight to fall on us. Many people within the Bible tried to do that, starting with Adam and Eve.

It cost them dearly.

But the ones who understood the true position of God in the big picture of their lives were the ones who achieved true greatness.

The Hall of Fame of Greatness

To me, it is sheer joy to see what ordinary people accomplished when they put their lives in the hands of their extraordinary God. Their accomplishments are so magnificent that it's easy to make the mistake of categorizing them in a league of their own. But that wouldn't be being accurate with the facts, and it would diminish the glory that God deserves for how He empowered these ordinary people to become truly great. Let's look at a few.

Abraham

God asked Abraham to leave the comfort and security of his home in Ur (in present-day Iraq) and follow God's lead to a sliver of land near the Mediterranean Sea. Actually, the vision wasn't that specific. God just said that He was giving Abraham a land far away and that He was going to make a great nation out of him.

With only a few exceptions, Abraham kept his eyes on God and kept his focus on God's plan. When he got to the land, he didn't quibble with his nephew, Lot, about who got the best grazing rights. That's because Abraham wasn't a scarcity thinker. He just kept entrusting himself to God.

God promised to make a great nation out of the union of Abraham and his wife, Sarah. Even after she was well past childbearing age, God honored Abraham's faith with the birth of their son, Isaac.

Abraham is known as the father of the Jewish race. He didn't gain that great position because of heritage or wealth or personal skill. He got it because he let God have preeminence in his life. He was a simple man who put God first in his life.

Joseph

It's easy to think that Joseph was some brilliant, bigger-than-life character who leveraged his superior intellect against the weaknesses of the members of his dysfunctional family. Actually, Joseph was just a young man who kept God in first position in his life. He didn't ask for or orchestrate any of the things that came his way. He just put God first when they did.

One disappointing thing after another happened that would have caused a lot of kids to turn their backs on the Lord, but these things only fueled Joseph to a greater level of trust. When his brothers sold him into slavery, Joseph had no idea whether he would ever see them again. But he kept his focus on God. When he was purchased by the Egyptian nobleman Potiphar, his commitment to true greatness caused him to go above and beyond the call of duty. He had a passionate love for God that showed itself in an unquenchable love and concern for people. This enabled him to be moved into a position of great responsibility in Potiphar's house.

When Potiphar's lonely wife came on to Joseph, it would have been easy to abandon his moral principles. After all, he was a long way from home. Who would know? But Joseph maintained his integrity, and his obedience to God got him thrown into prison on a false claim of sexual assault.

Unfazed, Joseph kept entrusting himself to God for protection and courage. He became the most responsible and reliable inmate in the jail. All along and without his knowledge, God was moving the props and players on the stage so that Joseph could someday save his people, Israel.

And we can't forget that moment when Joseph, promoted to a position equivalent to the prime minister of Egypt, saw the brothers who sold him into slavery. He could have easily finished them off. But he didn't seek revenge. He forgave them, as God expected him to, and used his position instead to bless them.

Joseph was great not because he was clever or at the right place at the right time. He was great because he put God first and let God have complete control of his life.

Ruth

When you've lost your husband, there's a famine in the land, your mother-in-law is depressed, and you're given the opportunity to cut your losses and go home, logic says that the decision should be obvious. But Ruth was committed to the God of her deceased husband, her mother-in-law, and the nation of Israel. And though she did not have Jewish blood running through her veins, Ruth had a Jewish heart beating in her chest.

God had a plan for Ruth, but she had no idea what it was. She was not making her moves based on some holy hunch that she was going to be the grandmother of the great King David and matriarch of the Messiah. There was no way she could have known that. She just knew that obedience to the God of Israel called for her to be faithful and caring toward her mother-in-law. Her complete trust in God put her in the position to be claimed by the next of kin to her deceased husband. Because Ruth trusted God, she went from obscurity to prominence, from poverty to stability, and from a widow to one of the key members of God's Hall of Greatness.

David

When this shepherd boy arrived at the battle lines to check on his brothers, he was not planning on killing Goliath and becoming a national hero. He performed so well that day because he arrived there with God in the forefront of his mind. That's the way David lived his life. When he looked across the valley at the Philistine army and the taunting nine-and-a-half-foot giant, he didn't see an overwhelming threat. He saw a disgusting insult to the God of Israel. Young David was the only one on his side of the battle line who realized that this conflict wasn't about nations, soldiers, giants, or shepherds with slingshots. It was about God. That's why he didn't hesitate to step up and face the giant in the power of the Lord.

We celebrate David's life, not because he was well educated, artistic, or well connected. There were lots of soldiers in Israeli uniforms that day who had these same assets. These assets would have had no bearing on the outcome. We celebrate his life because he walked onto a battlefield thinking, *This is not about me. This isn't about my life, or my safety, or my reputation.* He knew the challenge that Goliath made was against the God of the universe. And it was *that* God who empowered David when he slew the giant.

David was the starting point of a royal line that would culminate in the birth of the King of kings and the Lord of lords. Just as an obscure shepherd would face off against a giant of a man, an obscure carpenter's son would face off against a giant curse of sin. David didn't realize it at the time, but his exploits on the battlefield would make him a man for all seasons.

True, David had serious lapses in judgment. And everyone recognizes that King David's feet of clay cost him and his family dearly. But words weren't wasted on David when God called him "a man after his own heart" (1 Samuel 13:14). Even with these lapses, David still lived an extraordinary life from start to finish and is considered one of the great heroes of the Bible.

Esther

There is no doubt this young Jewish girl was a physical standout. When a beauty pageant was held to find a replacement for the queen of the empire, Esther put the competition to shame. She would have been on the cover of *People* magazine's "most beautiful women" issue.

But Esther is not considered one of the great women of the Bible because of her looks. She holds that position because she was willing to put God first in her life. When an edict was passed that set a date for the annihilation of the Jewish people, Esther put everything on the line. Her cousin Mordecai recognized her legitimate fears, but he reminded her that her God was simply using the assets that He had given her in advance to put her in a position to rescue His people (and hers). "Who knows," said Mordecai, "but that you have come to royal position for such a time as this?" (Esther 4:14).

Esther stepped up to Mordecai's challenge and put God in the forefront of her actions. She knew going in that the fickle nature of the emperor could cost her life. But she went anyway, saying, "If I perish, I perish" (v. 16).

Queen Esther was truly great because she lived her life in obedience to her mighty God. She was great because when the pressure was on, she realized, "It's not about me."

Daniel

Think of the conditions. You're just a teenager, and you've been separated from your family and carted off into captivity. You will probably never see your homeland again. You have been singled out to become one of the emperor's patsies. If you simply do what you're told and keep your personal preferences to yourself, you'll probably be able to live a quiet life and die an old man. If you voice even a single word of concern, your head could very likely end up in a jar on the king's desk.

Daniel was an orthodox Jew. That meant he was kosher. But the food the king of Babylon had allotted for him did not align with his Hebrew diet. He wasn't concerned that he had to study in the pagan schools of Babylon. He was grounded enough in his faith that he could separate truth from hogwash when it came to history, arts, science, and religion. But he could not compromise his dietary convictions. God was first with him. And because God was first with Daniel, he was first with God.

God honored Daniel's faithfulness as well as his courage. Few men in history enjoy the kind of place among God's greats as Daniel. He was smart, affable, organized, and gifted. But he didn't gain his place of prominence because of these life skills. He arrived there because he put God first in his life. For Daniel, it wasn't about Daniel. It was always about God.

Common Traps That Hinder True Greatness

In this chapter, I've listed some of the most familiar heroes of the Bible. But there are hundreds of honorable mentions who could also be named. They were men and women from every walk of life. Some were born to privilege, while others were birthed in

> Attributes are just attributes until they are put in the hands of a mighty God.

poverty. Some had the equivalent of an Ivy League head start; others arrived at their level of greatness simply by showing up. Some were smart; others were slow. Some were clever; others were dim. Some were attractive; others were plain. Some were athletic; others were awkward. But here's the important thing: *none* of these factors played a determining role in their greatness.

One proof can be found in the fact that the list of those who have been dishonorably discharged from God's service is crowded with people who have these same attributes. Attributes are just attributes until they are put in the hands of a mighty God. It is then that they move to assets that produce true greatness.

This is where so many parents miss their best opportunity to raise kids whose lives really count. They put too much emphasis on the things that have no bearing on whether the child achieves true greatness. They put too much emphasis on the head and not enough on the heart. They emphasize the superficial rather than the supernatural.

Here are some common misunderstandings of God that hinder kids from achieving true greatness:

God in a Jar—God is someone we encounter only on Sundays in church.

Kids in these families grow up viewing God as a casual outsider looking in.

God the Spare Tire—God is our last resort in emergencies.
Kids in these families learn that God's role is to help us when we need Him; otherwise, He's stored away for safekeeping.

God the Hitchhiker—God is some stranger we've picked up along the way.
Kids in these families think that He's just along for the ride but has no real say in where they are going.

God the Sugar Daddy—God is only there to dole out blessings.
Kids in these families only turn to God when their personal agenda doesn't turn out the way they planned.

God the "Heavy"—God is the artillery to "guilt" our children into submission.
Kids in these families often struggle with disgrace and sometimes reject their parents' faith.

The common denominator of parents who raise kids for true greatness is that God *is* their life. They live their lives for His glory. Every compartment of their lives is saturated with His presence and power.

They don't prioritize their lives the way so many people do: God, my spouse, my kids, my friends, my work, my church, and so on. No. Instead, they prioritize their lives this way: there's God, and then there's God and my spouse, God and my kids, God and my friends, God and my work, God and my church, God and my joys, God and my setbacks, God and every person and challenge I encounter each day.

When kids are brought up by parents whose hearts beat for God's glory, they are far more inclined to grow up to have hearts that beat for Him too.

The Upside to Putting God First

At this point you might be thinking that perhaps you'd rather raise a kid for something less than true greatness, because it sounds as if true greatness has little to offer your children personally. It's so much about God that it appears they are just bit players in His grand and sovereign schemes. You'd rather pursue a plan that at least gives your children a chance to do well financially, have some fun, and maybe make a name for themselves along the way.

If you're thinking that, maybe you ought to do a quick inventory of that list of names from the Hall of Greatness we listed above. These were people who did extremely well financially. They used their education in phenomenal ways. They were considered some of the most attractive and admired people of their generation. With the exception of David, they had fabulous relationships with their spouses and children.

And these only represent the tip of the iceberg if you are narrowing your review to just the great people in the Bible. When you expand your list to include the people who were considered truly great in history, or even in our current society, you quickly see that the fastest and surest way to set up your children for a phenomenal success track as an adult is to help them get their hearts and minds totally centered on God. That's because people who put God first are the most *valuable* people in society.

That means in every dimension of life they stand to gain the most because they offer the most to everyone and everything that they are involved in. Putting God first helps them make abundant thinking part of their relational DNA. Kids who eat, sleep, drink, think, walk, and talk God are the most *balanced* people in society. It is balance that assures their long-term greatness. It is balance that keeps parents from falling into the popular practice of raising one-dimensional kids—kids who are extremely good at one or two things but lack the continuity it takes to sustain long-term success.

It doesn't matter how talented, smart, handsome, pretty, or networked your children are if they don't know how to keep all of the pieces of their lives connected in a balanced way. Whatever successes they achieve will be overshadowed by the disappointments they experience that they are ill equipped to handle. There is only one person who knows how to bring it all together.

Jesus.

Hearts that are focused on Christ and fueled by His grace operate with a completely different attitude than hearts that only give lip service to Him. Attitudes lead to actions. Greatness shows itself in grace. Grace leads to humility and gratefulness. These attitudes create generous people who live to serve others. When it's not about us, there's no stopping the greatness God can pull off through our children.

It's a Process, Not an Event

Kids are far more likely to embody as adults what has been modeled to them through their childhood. None of us bats a thousand when it comes to serving God. We have our moments when we sometimes fall or fail. Assuming we are quick to acknowledge our mistakes, God is always quick to forgive. Allowing God's grace to dominate our thinking might come in spurts in the early part of our journey with Him. But the more we make it our aim to put Him first, the easier it is to do it on a regular basis. After a prolonged period of time, grace-based greatness can become second nature to you.

In the same way, it's realistic to assume that your children are more inclined to *grow into* this attitude than simply adopt it as a lifestyle from the get-go. Be patient with them. Don't "guilt" them. Just keep setting the example. It might take years or even decades before you see the fruit of your efforts. But it will be worth it. For in this single area of their lives, you have transferred to their hearts the most important part of the recipe for true greatness.

God wants to honor your devotion by welcoming you home to heaven someday. The first thing He wants to be able to say to you is, "Well done, good and faithful servant! You have been faithful with a few things; I will put you in charge of many things. Come and share your master's happiness!" (Matthew 25:23).

Most Christian parents want their kids to grow up with uncompromised commitment to put God first in their lives. They especially want their kids to demonstrate this attitude when this commitment is put to a real-life test.

You teach your children to be leaders, to have unblemished

ethics, and to be willing to take a stand for righteousness regardless of the price tag. You acknowledge that your kids have needs,
urges, and fragile feet of clay, but in spite of that, you encourage
them to put God first in their lives. You're hoping they'll
embrace this commitment by the time they become adults.

Every once in a while, however, God gives you reason to
believe that your efforts might pay off sooner rather than later.
Sometimes you have to find out how He's doing it through the
back limbs of the grapevine.

A mother of a girl in our church gave my wife, Darcy, a call
a couple of months ago. It seems that our youngest son had
invited a few of his friends from school over to hang out at our
house. The entourage was three guys and three girls. Her
daughter was one of the girls. In the process of their sitting
around and visiting, one of the kids mentioned that a mutual
friend of theirs, who also has a home in our neighborhood, was
having some friends over and had invited our son's group to
stop by. It was about ten thirty. They decided to go make an
appearance at the friend's get-together.

When they arrived, the front door was ajar. They'd figure out
later that the friend's parents weren't home. They went in,
assuming that everyone was either in the TV room or in the
backyard. Our son called out. His friend yelled back from the
den for them to come on in. Our son was leading the group.
But when he got to the doorway, he immediately sensed that
something wasn't right about the setting. He stopped short,
forcing the others to have to hold up in the hallway and not be
able to see what was going on.

The room was pitch-dark. Sixteen teenagers—eight boys
and eight girls—were crowded onto the various couches,

watching the big-screen television. But this wasn't a normal movie from Blockbuster entertaining the troops. Instead, it was a hard-core porn movie filling up the screen. The couple on the screen were having sex in high definition. Somewhere from the dark room, the boy welcomed my son and invited him and his friends to join them.

Sometimes you only get a split second to arrive at a moment of truth. All you've been taught and all you supposedly believe are placed before you in a single decision. Fortunately, the choice for my son came instantaneously. He saw the images on screen and then looked quickly at the faces of the people who were sitting on the couches. Without hesitation, he said, "This isn't a movie I care to watch. We're going back to my house." And then he saw one of his good friends right in the middle of the group. He looked directly at him, called his name, and said, "You're coming with me. You'll thank me tomorrow."

His friend got up and followed our son and his friends down the hall, out the door, and through the neighborhood to our house. But here's what was amazing: within minutes, every last teenager from that house was over at ours.

Sometimes, people are just looking for someone to show them how to live their lives better. You might be surprised how quickly your willingness to make God your master could be used to strengthen your child's resolve to make Him their master too.

And there are a lot of their friends who just might thank you in the morning.

Ten Ways to Be a Great Neighbor
(For Parents)

1. Be a good friend to all of your neighbors, not just the ones who align with your value system or your spiritual convictions.
2. Keep your yard and the outside of your house looking sharp. Never allow your house to bring a negative appearance to the neighborhood. Keep it painted, the grass cut, and the landscaping both up-to-date and maintained.
3. Pray for your neighbors, especially the ones who are the most difficult.
4. As much as possible, be quick to help your neighbors with things they are doing on their house, yard, or car—or with things they are struggling with in their lives.
5. Be friendly, kind, and encouraging whenever and wherever you encounter your neighbors.
6. Refuse to get pulled into neighborhood gossip. Living on a block with a bunch of desperate housewives is no fun for anyone.
7. Be especially encouraging to your neighbors' children—especially the kids who come from homes that might be overstressed (as a result of debt, marital difficulties, or lack of spiritual direction). Don't avoid the families

whose kids are out of control. You may have to limit their involvement with your children, but that doesn't mean you turn your back on their needs.

8. Welcome all new neighbors: whether married, divorced, single, cohabitating, gay, or straight. They are your neighbors. God put you near them to show His love, grace, and mercy. Invite them over to your home for dinner soon after they get settled. Make them feel welcome and safe.

9. Refuse to play the comparison game. Be genuinely happy for all the good things that happen in your neighbors' lives (new cars, new furnishings, a raise at work, a great accomplishment of a family member, etc.).

10. Be ready to weep and mourn with your neighbors when life doesn't go their way.

chapter eight

HELPING YOUR CHILDREN CHOOSE A GREAT MATE FOR LIFE

The best thing you can do to help your kids choose a great mate in life is to surround their childhood with grace. Create a family reputation for humility, gratefulness, generosity, and a servant attitude—and watch what shows up on the horizon. If misery loves company, then I can guarantee you that true greatness loves it too. And just as broken people tend to gravitate to broken people, truly great people tend to gravitate to others who share their value system. Especially when it comes to the person you want to share your most intimate moments with.

Darcy and I saw this up close and personal in a girl who crossed our paths shortly after we came out of graduate school. She wasn't glamorous, but she was pretty in a classic kind of way. Yet for reasons that seldom add up, guys never gave her the time of day when she was in high school. Come to think of it, none came calling in college or through the bulk of the decade of her twenties.

She never got to go shopping with her mother for a prom dress. There are no pictures of her with some high school boy in a rented tuxedo. No string of old boyfriends, bundles of well-read love letters, or deep conversations with her diary about the "crush" of the week. She probably could have bought a little help from the beauty parlor, but that wasn't her style. She was more of a "what you see is what you get" kind of lady, which is rather refreshing in the world of nip-and-tuck femininity. Besides, with the problems she had to contend with in her dysfunctional family, she wanted to draw as little attention to her physical features as possible.

When Darcy and I first got to know her, she was a junior in high school and had just recently decided to make God the master of her life. It was obvious that God owned her. This wallflower became a disciplined and conscientious follower of Jesus.

Her love for God showed most in her attitude. For a person who had so little to smile about at home and less to smile about in her social life, she carried a consistently upbeat outlook. Not to say that she didn't shed her share of tears. She certainly did. But most of the time, her tears were for others. That's because in the process of making God the master of her life, she had taken the logical next step and decided to let God dictate her mission in life as well. She lived for God and for others. And not just on Sunday or when it was convenient. Hers was a full-out devotion that permeated every dimension of her life. She was already on the fast track to greatness by the time she graduated from high school.

Our paths continued to cross after she finished college and began the process of carving out her niche in the marketplace. But during this time, her social calendar remained blank. She served God with her friends. She was available, encouraging, and gracious to everyone—both guys and girls alike. And she had a solid list of guys she could call friends. But no man stepped forward to see if she wanted to perhaps go out for coffee and discuss the past, the present, or—more important—the future.

Part of my heart ached for her, because I had grown to love her like a daughter or a younger sister. You know that feeling. You see what a wonderful person someone is and you know from your own experience how much joy a lifelong relationship would bring to her. But it simply would not materialize.

She played such a key role in the early lives of our children that Darcy and I saw her as an extension of our actual family. Each time she came into our world, we sensed the line on our spiritual and emotional stock value going up. She was always interested in us and our children, always encouraging, always desiring to make our lives better.

I don't know how many times Darcy and I said to each other, "When some guy finally wakes up and notices her, she is going to take his potential into the ionosphere." That's what happens when a person with God as her master and a bigger-than-life mission teams up with someone who has the same. There is no containing the horsepower that such a union creates.

I remember the day when she and I had one of those candid conversations that you'd prefer to avoid. Somehow the subject turned to matrimony . . . and her lack of it. It was not something I preferred to talk with her about, as I assumed it was a sensitive issue. But I remember clearly that when we broached the subject of marriage, her eyes twinkled, her face lit up, and a confident smile took center stage. She said, "Oh, I'm not worried. I'm going to be married. God's given me a clear comfort in my heart about it. I'm just waiting on Him to introduce me to my future husband. In the meantime, I'm doing everything I can to make sure that when that happens, I'm the best possible woman I can be for him."

That is the mind-set of a person who knows how to make one of the three most important decisions in life. Master, mission, and mate—they weave together to make one complete life, but only if each question is answered properly. How we prepare our children for this huge decision in life is merely a natural extension of how we prepared them for the other two.

Finding the Love of Your Life

One of the greatest points of anxiety in a person's life surrounds the process of dating, courting, and marrying whom they hope is the right person. So much of the pain of this process can be eliminated in advance by preparing our children properly. Most of the anxiety that people feel in this area is either self-imposed or forced on them by our culture. This decision doesn't need to be causing so much apprehension.

The key to finding the right mate is being the right person.

I don't want to make this process sound like it's simple, but it certainly isn't as difficult as most people make it. Once again, our culture takes something that God meant to be a rewarding part of everyone's life and complicates it beyond logic. Many people seem to be bent on finding a mate who meets their expectations and complements their ego needs. This selfish approach to marriage is part of the reason we have such staggering divorce statistics. The key to making this decision well is not so much in finding the person who can complete us but in becoming the kind of person who automatically makes the one we marry much more valuable.

Old sayings can be bru-
tal, but they can also save
us a lot of grief if we're
willing to learn from them.
One that is as true as the
gospel itself goes like this:

> The key to finding the right mate is being the right person.

"You're either doubled or halved on your wedding day." I know how accurate this is. That's because I was quadrupled on my wedding day. And although I sometimes joke that Darcy was bottom-fishing when she caught me, the truth is that she never would have married me if she hadn't seen in me the desire to put God first and others second. At the time, it wasn't a sophisti-cated commitment, and I often fell short of my personal goals. But it was there nonetheless. It was this criterion that Darcy felt was nonnegotiable when it came to marriage. Had I not made that commitment, I wouldn't have gotten much past the second date.

We had the normal physical attraction that young couples have, but it was secondary to a much greater priority: namely, who is the master of your life, and what's your mission in life going to be? Because both Darcy and I shared the same heart when it came to how we answered these questions, our decision to wed was not that difficult. Each of us wanted to team with someone who would multiply our ability to love God and care for people.

That is not to say that we were at the same level of maturity spiritually. We weren't. My commitment to God was real, but it did not compare to Darcy's steady, disciplined focus. But the spiritual raw material was clearly evident, and she considered my track record as she made the decision to team her heart with mine. These factors made our wedding day a date on which our individual potential took a giant leap to a new level.

I read somewhere that a Draft horse can pull two tons by itself. Harness it with another Draft horse, and the two can pull six tons. There's something about merging our gifts and skills with the right person that gives both a compounded potential. That's why helping your children choose to let God be the master of their lives, as well as letting God dictate their mission in life, raises the chances that they will allow God to direct them to mates who share these same convictions.

When I think back to my own wedding day, I realize how none of the things that our culture considers priorities were compelling factors . . . with the exception of one—I thought then (and still think now) that Darcy was the most beautiful woman I had ever laid eyes on. Physical attraction isn't a negative when you're talking about the union of two people who have chosen to make God the master of their lives. We would hope that most couples getting married find each other physically appealing.

The problem is when we let the world's priorities of beauty color our standard. That's because the world system doesn't have a clue when it comes to the role that physical attraction plays in the big picture of a great marriage. The world emphasizes a much more superficial view of physical attraction, one that measures sex appeal, sexual experience, arbitrary physical features, and whether a person measures up to current standards of style. The utter folly of these criteria is that they cannot sustain a lousy relationship. Every day, some of the world's most beautiful and stylish people stand before the divorce judge to figure out who is going to get to keep the cappuccino machine.

On our wedding day, Darcy and I were attracted to each other, but our physical attraction wasn't the main reason we wanted to cast our lots with each other. We both wanted to live for God. Our wedding day simply made it possible for us to blend our goals, dreams, and talents into a union that multiplied us exponentially.

When We Unwittingly Undermine God's Best for Our Kids

Before we look at some of the things we can do to help our children make a wise choice in this department, let's look at some of the things we might want to try avoiding. It's easy to slip over some thin lines in our coaching and put wrong priorities in our kids' heads.

Prioritizing Physical Features

If Dad is fixating on the cheerleaders who are dancing during a break in the action of an NBA game, his children are learning that, at least from their father's perspective, sex appeal matters. I'm not suggesting that godly fathers should be blind to the obvious, but that doesn't mean we have to worship it. When we do, it elevates sexual charisma as a higher priority in our children's minds than it deserves to be.

Moms have to be careful too. When you're sitting in a restaurant with your daughter and an attractive young man goes by, and you say something like, "Oh my, will you check him out? He's cute!" Sorry, Mom, but you just told your daughter that something as temporary and superficial as how a guy looks in tight-fitting clothes is a high priority. It is the stuff of the *heart* that sustains a relationship, not the fleeting features of youth.

Obviously, our kids can lean toward the world's priority of sexual attraction without any help from us. It's part of the hormone-saturated lives they lead during their young years. But we need to be careful not to give this built-in frustration any unnecessary fuel.

Here's the good news. Kids committed to true greatness have an internal stewardship when it comes to their bodies. They tend to take better care of themselves, eat more conscientiously, exercise, and pace themselves better. They have less of the wear and tear of anxiety on their faces. They not only tend to look more wholesome when they are young, but they also tend to age more gracefully. Why? It's simply the outside of their bodies reflecting the inner attitude of their hearts.

Prioritizing a Family's Economic Pedigree

There have been uncountable ballads sung and movies made about young lovers who try to unite families on opposite sides on the social or economic ladder. Most of the time, the problem is with the parents, not the young lovers. Are differing economic backgrounds a factor when it comes to two people getting married? Absolutely! Should it be a deal killer? Absolutely not! There are myriad factors that require attention and adjustments when it comes to two people from different types of families getting married. But these are easily processed when they slip through the common filter of lives that are sold out to Christ. That's why parents who make a big deal out of this often send selfish as well as arrogant messages to their children's hearts.

To think that someone has better potential as a marriage partner simply because he or she comes from a wealthy family is ludicrous. It's dangerous too. It just might get our children thinking there is some actual truth to this. There isn't. There are healthy families on all rungs of the economic ladder. Crowded on those same rungs is an even distribution of unhealthy families too. Marriageability is determined not by economics but by where a person stands with God.

We must be very careful not to disparage a person one of our kids is interested in just because he or she might come from the wrong side of the tracks. Remember, that's where Jesus grew up. Some of His finest servants learned how to catch fish on that side of the tracks too. Oh, and lest I forget, some of the wealthiest titans of industry grew up over there also. Where a person is raised and whether or not he or she enjoyed an upper-middle-class childhood are no indications of how well he or she will do economically.

> Marriageability is determined not by economics but by where a person stands with God.

Darcy and I are a great example of this. Darcy's family lived on the edge of poverty when she was a very young girl. But her father was a resourceful man with an incredible drive. He ultimately moved his family to Washington, D.C., so that he could take a position among the power brokers who crowded the halls and chambers of Capitol Hill. When I met her, she was from a solid middle-class family. Her father carried a briefcase to work and spent his days in crisp, starched shirts and silk ties.

When Darcy got to know me, my family was holding as tightly as we could to the bottom rung of the middle class. My father wore blue collars to work. While Darcy's father took lunch in the Senate cafeteria, my father opened a lunch box on the tailgate of his truck. While Darcy's dad fulfilled his role as a professional staff member of the Senate Appropriations Committee, my father might be in a crawl space under a house, trying to install a piece of ductwork. The difference in our economic backgrounds was simply a factor that we had to process once we were married—nothing more.

Prioritizing Earning Potential

It is tempting to push our children toward prospective mates who are preparing for a professional life that has a reputation for great income. When you hear that the person your child is interested in is in medical or law school, it's easy to think that this person is a much better match than, say, someone preparing to do social work, be a tradesman or a teacher, or perhaps go to the mission field. Let's be honest. We all want our children, especially our daughters, to be in a situation where they don't have to worry about their next meal or how they are going to make ends meet. Fortunately, when God is their master and they have the qualities of true greatness, they'll be *fine*. Unfortunately, many parents who have achieved a degree of success find that success not only clouds their judgment but also erases a lot of their memory. Many successful parents forget that they had little to nothing when they got married.

When Darcy and I got married, I had paid for two months' rent in advance, paid for my first semester of graduate school in advance, and owned a 1966 Pontiac GTO; we had $325 *between* us. As we crossed the country from our wedding to our honeymoon at Dallas Theological Seminary, we pulled behind us the smallest U-Haul trailer that you could rent. It contained the sum total of our earthly possessions.

We didn't consider ourselves poor at the time (although all of the U.S. government standards for evaluating poverty would have put us in that category). We were simply on the front side of what we assumed was going to be a very productive life as a couple. We had a plan. On top of that, we figured our character, determination, and work ethic gave us unlimited earning potential. We weren't wondering *if* we would make it economically. We were simply ready to see which way God would empower us to do so.

When you coach your children to prioritize earning potential when choosing a person to marry, you could push them into the arms of a person whom God never intended for them. On top of that, your children's focus on earning potential could block them from the path that He clearly meant for them to follow in life. That path may not be strewn with six- or seven-figure incomes and a summer cabin at the lake. But if it is the path God wants them to follow, He will provide everything they need. God is a thorough sustainer. He clearly leads some couples to pursue professions that may not pay high-end salaries, but He puts them in the best position to fulfill His plan for their personal greatness.

In his book *The Millionaire Mind*, Thomas J. Stanley researched whether there is any correlation between financial success and the earning potential of one of the spouses of a truly wealthy couple. His findings may surprise you:

> It is a popular notion—if you want to become wealthy, just marry a millionaire. Or you can marry the son or daughter of a millionaire couple. Eventually your spouse will inherit a pot of gold, and you assume, your husband or wife will share it with you. . . . The data strongly indicates that neither of these hypotheses is true. . . . Most millionaires did not select their spouse because of his or her wealth characteristics. Nor were they initially attracted to their husbands or wives because their parents "had money." In fact, the wealth factor was not even rated by our millionaires as an important quality of a spouse that contributed to a successful marriage.[1]

Dr. Stanley goes on to show from his data that the biggest factor contributing to the earning potential of the vast number of millionaires he studied was the *length* of their marriages. Longevity in a marriage correlates directly with the health within that union. Earning potential has nothing to do with healthy marriages. Tons of high-income marriages break up. Therefore, one of the best things we can do as parents is to equip our children to marry the right person, not the best fiscal candidate. We need to focus on the best priorities in a mate: grace, humility, gratefulness, generosity, and a servant attitude.

Keep in mind, if the kids standing at the altar are doing what God wants them to do, what more could a righteous parent want? Besides, when it comes to long-term wealth, the Bible says that God is preparing a place for us. In fact, Jesus said, "Do not let your hearts be troubled. Trust in God; trust also in me" (John 14:1).

Keep in mind, too, that wealth has far less to do with earning potential and everything to do with practicing biblical laws of stewardship. Regardless of the earning potential of your child's mate, they can do just fine financially if they are careful to follow God's laws when it comes to money He entrusts to them.

Lest we forget. I want to mention the primary reason truly great people have better marriages and enjoy more economic success. Two words: "low maintenance." People who are humble, grateful, generous, and have a servant attitude are naturally balanced when it comes to day-to-day challenges. They are easier to live with, to laugh with, and to love on. They don't run up irrational debt or *need* to live extravagant lives. Their egos aren't out of control which makes them quick to process conflict. If you want to set your child up to enjoy a peaceful, passionate, and productive marriage relationship, just raise them for true greatness.

The Dilemmas of Falling in Love

When it comes to practical partnerships, Dr. Norman Wright offers a great checklist for potential health in a marriage. Traits like flexibility, empathy, the ability to work through tough problems, the ability to give and receive love, emotional stability, similar values in the family of origin, having common interests, and honoring communicative skills are the things that you want to look for when deciding whom to spend the rest of your life with.[2]

I don't want to be too simplistic here, but there is an overriding factor to which all these traits are subordinate. Actually, it's not an "it"; it's a "who." His name is Jesus. When a couple considering marriage submit themselves to God as their ultimate and singular master, and they share the mission to love God and serve others, it is amazing how those two choices can trump any of the extenuating circumstances that might question the wisdom of their union. That's because people who are serving God and living for Him are more inclined to empty themselves of their selfish agendas and put God's love, mercy, and grace in place instead.

That's not to say that a major problem in any of the traits on Dr. Wright's list should be ignored, but if your child's future mate has a passionate love for God that shows itself in an unquenchable love and concern for others, he or she likely has the internal equipment to address these problems.

All this said, the best wedding gift we can give our children is to show them what a great married couple looks like. Few areas of our children's lives are as formatted for goodness or for ill as the example we set in our marriage.

At this point, I know some of you are saying, "Well, that's just great! I've read all this way only to find out that my divorce has ruined my chances of helping my child make a wise choice on his [or her] wedding day." Actually, God's grace assumes that we all struggle to put forth the example that we'd prefer. All marriages have conflict. All couples fight. Sometimes the conflict ends in divorce. But a divorce doesn't mean that parents have lost the chance

> The best wedding gift we can give our children is to show them what a great married couple looks like.

to positively influence their kids when it comes to choosing their mates. It simply means that we must factor in the downside of the divorce on our children's lives and then balance it off with grace-filled candor.

If you are divorced, you need to forgive your ex and move on with your life. Regardless of what your ex may be doing to you, you need to show your children how to respond in return with love and grace (as Jesus does with us when we are difficult to love). I'm not suggesting that you roll over and play dead and let an out-of-control ex destroy you or the kids. But however you deal with your ex, do it without rage in your demeanor or revenge in your heart. Vengeance is God's job. Let Him settle the score.

The apostle Paul put the truth on the bottom shelf when it comes to this issue of dealing with people who are trying to work you over. He says:

> Do not repay anyone evil for evil. Be careful to do what is right in the eyes of everybody. If it is possible, as far as it depends on you, live at peace with everyone. Do not take revenge, my friends, but leave room for God's wrath, for it is written: "It is mine to avenge; I will repay," says the Lord. On the contrary: "If your enemy is hungry, feed him; if he is thirsty, give him something to drink. In doing this, you will heap burning coals on his head." Do not be overcome by evil, but overcome evil with good. (Romans 12:17–21)

If you have gone through a divorce or are in a troubled marriage, you are in an excellent position to show your children what it's like to turn a life around and let God be your master by fulfilling His will for your life.

Helping Our Kids Process Their Humanness

Even the most conscientious Christian kids still struggle in a battle with their flesh. These battles are accentuated when they fall in love—especially if they feel they've met the person they want to spend the rest of their lives with. The grace we show them through this time can play a huge role in helping them make the right decision when it comes to their mates. It can also help them get there in the best possible shape morally.

Helping your children set the goal of being sexually pure on their wedding night is biblical, desirable, and doable. But many parents unwittingly make this goal an excruciating burden. This happens when we articulate the goal but do little or nothing to help them reach it. We usually do a good job of trying to enforce their purity, but that doesn't take into account the fact that they still have a desperate battle raging around them as well as *in* them. If all we give them are lectures about purity and guilt trips when they struggle, their chances of achieving this goal go way down. We need to be engaged in a continual, grace-based dialogue with them throughout their childhoods and adolescence.

It might help to know that the average teenage boy thinks about sex *all the time*! The average teenage girl thinks about sex a lot of the time. You can do your best to minimize their exposure to sexual stimuli, but don't be fooled into thinking this has won the lion's share of the battle.

I spent my younger years of childhood in western Pennsylvania. There was a truck stop my father often took me to for breakfast. When we pulled up, there were always a couple of Amish horses and buggies tied up outside. Without fail, when we'd walk by the magazine rack, there would be one or more Amish teenage boys looking at the *Playboy* and *Penthouse* magazines. Even one of the most cloistered spiritual societies on the globe can't keep their boys' raging hormones from getting the best of them.

That's why the prolonged cocooning of kids from the harmful culture around them often yields disappointing results. The reason is simple: the biggest battle for teenagers' purity rages *within* them, not around them. Their hormones are as potent as heroin, and they want to overtake and dominate your children's thoughts as well as their choices. Kids in controlled environments sometimes struggle more than kids who have moderate exposure to the world's messages.

Your child's moral purity has far more to do with the work of the Holy Spirit. Spiritually conscientious kids who are raised closer to the cultural conflict have no choice but to appropriate the Holy Spirit's power when it comes to maintaining moral purity. Every day, they must lean on Him for strength to overcome the urges within and the messages without. In a controlled environment, it's easy to assume that you are safer than you actually are. The protection that parents and kids often rely on is the man-made cocoon rather than the Holy Spirit.

I'm not suggesting that parents should throw their sons and daughters to the wolves. Conscientious parents realize that there is a balance that needs to be maintained when it comes to *protecting* and *preparing* their kids. We just need to know, however, that there are negative trade-offs if you stray too far in either direction. That's why we have to be savvy about understanding what effect the model we have chosen for our parenting has on our children.

We do our children a huge service if we walk them and talk them through their battle with their culture as well as their hormones. We shouldn't be surprised our daughters struggle with fantasy; we should assume it. The same thing goes when it comes to our sons. We shouldn't be shocked that they struggle with masturbation; we should assume that it is an ongoing battle. Notice that I used the word *shocked*. This is the absolute worst response we can have to our teenagers' struggles. If anything, it shows how naive we are about how they are wired and how selfish we are about our image.

Most parents don't want their children to surrender their honor to these battles (I know I sure don't). But at the same time, we must have a realistic and grace-based view of what we're dealing with. When a mom can be a safe sounding board for her daughter to discuss some of her erotic thoughts, and when a dad can provide a steady and safe haven for his son to discuss his struggles with lusts and masturbation, then these parents put themselves in the best position to coach their children through these struggles. Our kindness, love, and understanding enable them to gain not only wisdom but strength for the battle they are having.

All I'm suggesting is that we deal with our children's struggles the way God helps us deal with ours. We can always go to God with our battles, our guilt, and our shame. The more our children find a similar response from us when it comes to their moral struggles, the easier it will be for them to take these same struggles to God and gain victory over them through His power.

Cutting to the Chase

The layers of complexity that we wrap over the issue of our kids choosing their mates only get in the way of the best thing we can do to help them make a good choice. You can probably figure out what I'm going to say. The more we build the values of grace-based greatness into our children's hearts, the more likely that Mr. or Ms. Right will show up on their radar screens. Here's why. Kids who are sold out to God and have an unquenchable love and concern for others have a way of sensing when they are around kids who are not. That doesn't mean they see themselves as better. They just see themselves as moving through life to a completely different rhythm. This causes them to have a difficult time connecting romantically to a contrary heart.

This is a two-way street. Young men and women who are sold out to Christ tend to gravitate to kids who share the same values when it comes time to date and get married. There are exceptions, of course, but most of the time a little honesty shows that perhaps the child has not handed his heart over to God as much as his parents thought he had. Regardless, the best protection for a bad union is to help our children put God first.

Pastor Tommy Nelson, in his teachings on the Song of Solomon, advises that you should race as fast and as passionately toward God's heart as you can. Should you look out the corner of your eye and see a member of the opposite gender racing as passionately as you, you might want to give that person careful consideration when it comes to marriage.

The psalmist says, "Delight yourself in the LORD and he will give you the desires of your heart" (Psalm 37:4). It's one of those cause-and-effect verses. When people are delighting in the

Lord, the desires of their hearts tend to be put there by God. Young people willing to put God first take all the anxiety out of choosing the right mate for their future. Just keep trusting your heart to Him; He'll bring that person along in due time.

WHAT IF YOU DON'T HAVE A GREAT MARRIAGE?

Obviously, it is going to be difficult for you to expect your children to make a choice that you haven't made yourself. So what if you don't have a great marriage? Even if you didn't let God help you choose your mate when you got married, you need to let Him help you love your mate in order to stay married.

Remember what I said earlier: God is the God of the second chance and the clean slate. Just as He redeemed your heart from the sin that had condemned you, He can redeem your marriage from the unfortunate years that might have gone before. The question isn't, can God save my marriage? It's, will I let Him?

God Keeps His Promises

Remember the young lady I told you about at the opening of this chapter? She made God her master. She chose to let Him oversee her mission of using her entire life to glorify Him.

Her life was known for its humility, gratefulness, generosity, and servant attitude. All the while that she was delighting in God's goodness, He was putting a strong sense within her that she was going to be married. So she got herself ready . . . and then waited patiently for Mr. Right. She waited through all those years when her girlfriends were getting married. Undaunted, she stayed calm . . . and kept waiting. Remember, waiting in the Bible does not mean inactivity. It's about faith, calm, and confidence.

Fortunately, God didn't keep her waiting indefinitely. Just before she turned thirty, an amazing man came into her life. He, too, had made God the master of his life. He, too, had made it his mission to live his life for something bigger than life itself. He, too, had decided that he only wanted God's best for his marriage. He, too, had been waiting for God to make the introduction.

It's been more than a decade since their wedding. And it's been a marvelous decade to behold. These two were already great people when they fell in love. Since merging their lives, they have made *greatness* an inadequate word to describe their extraordinary love. It is a love that comes directly from the infinite reservoir within the heart of God. Their love has produced two fantastic sons. And God just keeps blessing them, using them, and filling them.

Our children have many paths they can take to get to the marriage altar. But there is only one path that allows them to enjoy a marriage committed to something bigger than life and love combined—the one that teams them with a person who shares their passion for God and their love and concern for others. It merges with the path that calls them to allow God to be the master of their lives and the path that encourages them to make living for others their absolute mission in life. These three paths converge to create a safe thoroughfare through life.

And they lead directly to true greatness.

Ten Ways to Teach Your Young Children to Put God First

1. Consistently read them stories at bedtime that tell about God's mighty power and love.
2. When a frightening or troubling situation comes up, gather them around and show them how to put themselves in God's hands through prayer.
3. Show them how to pray for those they love, as well as those who need God's love, every night at bedtime.
4. Welcome them each morning with a positive reminder of God's love and design for their lives. (An example: "This is another great day that God has given us to shine for Him. You have a wonderful personality, and it's going to be fun to see how God enables you to use it for Him today.")
5. Allow God's presence to become second nature in your everyday activities (such as praying at mealtime, pointing out wonders in nature, observing how God works in people around you, singing songs to Him, etc.).
6. Avoid evoking God's name in an intimidating manner to express displeasure with disobedience.

7. Make going to church and Sunday school a fun, happy, and nonnegotiable part of your family life.

8. Help your children hide God's Word in their hearts by memorizing key Scriptures that tell of God's love, mercy, grace, protection, and power.

9. Make kindness, sharing, and consideration for every member of the family a natural outgrowth of your love for God.

10. Avoid strong-arming your children to accept Christ as their Savior. Treat them the way God treats you (with grace), and let the Holy Spirit draw them to Himself on His timetable.

chapter nine

HELPING YOUR CHILDREN CHOOSE A GREAT MISSION IN LIFE

The club is called an Adams Tight Lie. If you're a golfer, you immediately recognize the name. Most men and women who play the game of golf usually have one or more of these clubs in their bag. Because of its shape and the way it displaces its weight, it's the perfect club for certain conditions.

I was looking at those conditions.

But first, you need to know that I was playing golf with my brother-in-law. He has this annoying habit of beating me most of the time. The other annoying habit he has is gloating after the fact.

I needed this hole.

We were playing a par 5. I had come out of my shoes on my drive, using every bit of my strength. I was sitting just off of the fairway in the rough. From where I stood, the fairway sloped down about 150 yards and then started a nice ascent for another 65 yards to the center of the green. The Tight Lie I held in my hands could make it there, provided I did one thing—hit the ball perfectly. When you do it, you know it before the ball leaves the club head.

I did it. I knew as my arms were following through on my swing that I was going to like the outcome. It turned out that I loved it. My ball rolled to a stop seven inches from the cup. I tapped in for the eagle, took a one-stroke lead, and maintained it for two more holes for the win.

There's nothing like it when all of the variables come together at once to create the perfect effect. It's called hitting the sweet spot.

Hitting the Sweet Spot

Did you know that very few people make a living doing what they enjoy? In fact, best-selling author Marcus Buckingham says that only about 20 percent of people in the marketplace are doing a job that they love.[1] That's a crying shame. To actually spend the bulk of the waking hours of your entire productive adult life doing something you don't enjoy, well, it's no wonder a lot of kids are reluctant to grow up. And we need to keep in mind that if 80 percent of working adults don't enjoy what they do for a living, then there is a very good chance our children are going to be part of that group.

Unless, of course, we send them into their adult lives with a mission bigger than just making a living. As life coach Ron Jensen says so well in the title of his book, we need to raise kids who know how to make a life, not just a living.[2]

Very few people figure out how to hit their sweet spot. Do you know what I'm talking about? It's when every dimension of life seems to be working in harmony to create a well-rounded and effective person. Hitting the sweet spot happens when who we are, what we do, whom we share our life with, and whom we live our life for align for a maximum sense of contentment. It's the phenomenon that helps us achieve our highest and best good in all areas of our lives. In sports, you always know when you hit the sweet spot. In life, you know it too.

> We need to raise kids who know how to make a life, not just a living.

Unfortunately, many parents think they need to complicate the process in order to succeed. They assume that hitting the sweet spot with your life requires years of serious self-sacrifice, a high level of academic prowess, and strategic connections in a network of movers and shakers. They assume that getting their children ready for a successful future requires that their children must do the same. I'm trying to think which expression best summarizes these assumptions.

Hogwash works fairly well.

God didn't make the goal of hitting our sweet spot difficult. As we have seen, Jesus said that He came so that we "may have life, and have it to the full" (John 10:10). Jesus wants us to enjoy our jobs, our spouses, our kids, our friends, our leisure, and all of the challenges that come with each of these categories of our lives. He wants us to have such an overwhelming sense of success running through our average day that we can even find purpose and meaning in our trials.

The apostle Paul put it this way: "We rejoice in the hope of the glory of God. Not only so, but we also rejoice in our sufferings, because we know that suffering produces perseverance; perseverance, character; and character, hope" (Romans 5:2–4).

God wants our children to grow up to live adult lives that are far more than just seeing how much money they can make and how well known they can become. He wants them to make a profound difference *eternally*. When we raise our children with this in the forefront of our efforts, we automatically focus on higher goals than fame, power, beauty, and wealth—goals that most parents assume are sovereign. We aim them at a true greatness that is bathed in grace and carried out through humility, gratefulness, generosity, and a servant attitude.

> The best childhood you could give your kids is a childhood filled with fun, excitement, laughter, and lots of grace.

When we aim at developing this higher standard for why our children are living their lives, these temporal goals tend to take care of themselves a lot more effectively as well as easily. In fact, many truly great kids grow up to enjoy more fame, power, beauty, and wealth than they could ever want. More important, they get to enjoy these great assets to adulthood in a more balanced and satisfying way.

I don't mean to imply that raising kids who embrace a great mission in life is simple. It's just not as complicated as we make it.

The best childhood you could give your kids is a childhood filled with fun, excitement, laughter, and lots of grace. Sure, they'll have to learn sacrifice. Obviously, they have lots of work they'll need to do, as well as responsibilities they'll need to maintain. These are standard features of the job description of someone who has made God the master of his or her life. But it doesn't have to be a heavy or foreboding experience.

Take their education, for instance. A good education is obviously important to your children's future, but it will not play the deciding factor when it comes to their having a great mission in life. And when it comes to a network of movers and shakers, there is only one person they have to be on a first-name basis with if they want all the right doors to open for them. His name is *Jesus*!

The more we instill a sense of true greatness into our children, the more likely their practical, day-to-day lives will fall into place. Conversely, our failure to do this almost guarantees that they'll never "hit the sweet spot" in life. If you want to play a key role in increasing the chances that your children grow up to have great jobs, get paid well for what they do, know how to accumulate and retain wealth, develop a high degree of influence, have an enjoyable marriage, and raise great kids, you'd do well to focus on instilling a great sense of mission into them. It is a great *mission* that will cause all of these other things to find their rightful places in your kids' lives.

> The more we instill a sense of true greatness into our children, the more likely their practical, day-to-day lives will fall into place.

A great mission happens when we help our children figure out that regardless of what they choose to do for a living, if they do it with a passionate love for God that shows itself in an unquenchable love and concern for the people that surround them, they will knock the ball out of the park. If they approach an honest vocation with an overriding sense of grace that is transferred through genuine humility, gratitude, generosity, and a servant attitude, the future belongs to them. And they can start practicing these characteristics right now in how they do their schoolwork, play on their athletic teams, mow the neighbor's grass, and babysit your friend's kids.

Slipping Off Course

How do we get off target when it comes to grooming our kids for greatness? Part of it goes back to the conventional wisdom we discussed in chapter 3. We work like crazy to build into them those things that lack the ability to cause true greatness (fame, power, beauty, and wealth). These things are extremely difficult and time-consuming to build into our children's lives, and they don't determine true greatness at all. So we stress ourselves to the limit, thinking that we are being conscientious parents for our children. But when we stress ourselves over preparing our children for adulthood, we stress them too.

There are a couple of areas where I feel that well-intended, even conscientious parents often undermine their own efforts. One is the incredibly high level of *expectations* we put on ourselves and our children. We set the goal of excellence in the areas of fame, power, beauty, and wealth, so much so that most of our children's early years are simply an ongoing reminder of how far below their best they are. Whether our expectations are for their grades, looks, weight, or relationships, these empty goals rule us when it comes to the unending evaluation we give our children. It's even worse when we spiritualize these things. If you tell your children that Jesus loves straight As and is disappointed with Bs and Cs, our children begin to think that they can never measure up to His expectations for them either. Spiritualizing the efforts your children put forth for things that don't determine greatness is a great way to set them up to reject God as a vital part of their future. If they assume that He's disappointed with them most of the time, then why bother?

While We're Talking About Grades

For the record, top grades and high SAT scores play little, if any, role in whether a child grows up to amass wealth. These things may help them get a higher-paying job. The fact is the average college student makes more money over a lifetime than the average high school graduate. The same can be said for the high school graduate when compared to the high school dropout. So education matters. But it has much less of an effect on whether or not our children end up with much to show for all of their efforts than we think.

In his book *The Millionaire Next Door*, Thomas J. Stanley points out that most people work to *appear* wealthy. But if you did an actual bottom-line analysis of their assets minus their liabilities, many of the people who appear wealthy are actually just a couple of paychecks away from financial annihilation. In Texas, they're referred to as "big hat, no cattle." The point behind the title of his book is that most of the truly wealthy people are living among us without flaunting their wealth.

They don't need to. They're secure.

They have other assets internally that make it possible for them to achieve great goals in the marketplace and be able to enjoy the benefits of these achievements in a balanced way. Guess what? Humility, gratefulness, generosity, and a servant attitude are just the kind of assets Dr. Stanley outlined that these people bring to their careers.

But while he's discussing America's wealthiest people, Dr. Stanley also puts academic achievement in perspective. In this book, he mentions the usual false assumptions people have about the way the average person achieves wealth (such as inheritance, luck, and stock market investments), and then he turns to the issue of academics:

> Topping the list [of false assumptions] would be high IQ, high SAT scores and grade point average in school, along with atten-dance at a top college or university. It may be difficult to dis-lodge this cherished myth from our thinking, but my survey of self-made millionaires disproves it. . . . The statistics demon-strate that a minority of millionaires whom I surveyed achieved high test scores or grades or went to top schools. These factors were probably useful to a small percentage of the millionaires, but most attained their high levels of economic productivity without those "assets."[3]

I'm not suggesting that we shouldn't help our children do as well as they can in school. But if we want them to achieve true greatness—and perhaps have something tangible to show for it—we'd be better off concentrating our efforts on helping them build a great sense of mission with their overall life rather than just with their skils.

The Anchor Tenets of a Great Mission in Life

In chapter 5, we established the "anchor tenets" of grace-based greatness: humility, gratefulness, generosity, and a servant attitude. We built a biblical case for them at that time. Let's spend a few minutes seeing what these tenets look like fleshed out in our children's daily lives. It will be easy to see how building these attributes into our children can't help but ensure success once they are part of the adult marketplace.

Humility

Kids with a mission to live great lives don't need praise and applause to feel complete. As we said in chapter 5, we should discourage arrogance, haughtiness, or bragging. Should applause come their way (because of some achievement or the exercising of their gifts or skills), we want to help them learn to respond to it graciously. This is a lot easier if we are raising them with the aim of giving them a secure love, a significant purpose, and a strong hope.

Some people confuse humility with a low view of themselves. They divert attention and praise from themselves because they feel unworthy to receive legitimate recognition for their efforts. This attitude is an insult to God. Jesus doesn't make junk, He didn't die for junk, and He certainly wouldn't waste His time trying to empower junk. The Bible says that we are "fearfully and wonderfully made" (Psalm 139:14). God has given us intrinsic value and extraordinary abilities. When we mine our intrinsic value and exercise our extraordinary abilities, we're most likely going to gain the approval of others.

People with a true sense of mission don't need this approval.

But they don't insult that approval should it aim its spotlight at them. When recognition or applause comes their way, they can acknowledge it, show appreciation for it, but refuse to bask in it—or worse, bathe in it. They do their best because it's the least they want to do when God is the core of their lives. Their gracious response to approval and their refusal to demand it only endear them more. In the end, humility makes them extremely *attractive and valuable.*

Gratefulness

When God is your master, and you realize that you've been bought and paid for with His blood, it only makes sense that you'd be grateful. But a lot of people don't follow this logic. In spite of all that they've been given, they aren't satisfied. They don't appreciate what they have, and they want more. Kids are born with a bent toward this type of attitude. Teaching them gratefulness is one of the greatest assets you can give them for living out a powerful mission in life.

One way to do this is to refuse to embrace the pervasive attitude of entitlement that so many people have. Lacking any sense of humility or graciousness, they believe they are deserving of the best seat in the house, the best office, the first place in line, the least amount of hassle, the biggest piece of the pie, the last piece of the pie, the best teachers for their kids, and the least amount of consequences for their kids' mistakes.

If we allow a "me first" attitude to gain a foothold in our children's lives, it will guarantee them a miserable future. Furthermore, if we model an attitude of entitlement, we will most likely look down the barrel of that gun when our kids bring their ungratefulness to bear on our lives.

When kids go into the future with a profound attitude of gratefulness, people are more inclined to better their situation. When they are thankful for their paychecks, their offices, their desks, their computers, their teams, and their jobs, the people around them automatically tend to think about them when it's time to improve any of these factors. And even if they are in an unreasonable environment with unkind people, they should still maintain an attitude of gratefulness and entrust themselves to the God they serve to look out on their behalf. An attitude of gratefulness makes people extremely *attractive and valuable* to the people who are in the best position to bless them.

Generosity

One of the most important attributes of consistently generous people is that they are careful stewards of their assets. Otherwise they can't maintain generosity as a lifestyle. Building generosity into your children requires that you also teach them how to pace themselves and handle their money properly. When they learn the laws of money that are built into the Bible, they can create the wealth that will enable them to be generous for a lifetime.[4]

But money is just one of the ways the truly great show generosity. They are generous with their time, their brainpower, their willpower, and their sweat. They bring this attitude both to work and to play. This attitude is never about doing the minimum or just getting by. And sure enough, people with generous attitudes become extremely *attractive and valuable* to the people and forces that surround them in the future.

Servant Attitude

"Servant attitude" is a way of saying all of the other assets in one breath. People who are humble, others-oriented, trustworthy, grateful, tenacious, courageous, compassionate, and generous are going to have a servant attitude.

A servant attitude starts with being God's servant. But that choice automatically extends into a servant attitude toward all whom God cares about. God primarily cares about people. Kids who are raised to make a wise choice about their mission in life are kids who learn to serve early. Whether it's helping the teacher pick up the toys at the end of Sunday school or taking an elderly neighbor's newspaper to her door every day, our children must learn a servant attitude by exercising a servant's heart as soon as they are capable of breathing on their own.

Because I've written a book entitled *Why Christian Kids Rebel*, I am often cornered by Christian parents who are struggling with a rebellious child.[5] This child might have been brought up in an idyllic spiritual environment, yet he or she shows no appreciation. After I've heard about the problem, I ask the parents where the child is presently serving, as well as where he or she has served in the past. I'm not asking about token acts of service that are done mostly to make the servers feel better about themselves (like a week-long foreign missions trip bracketed by fifty-one weeks of doing nothing for others), but rather those substantive areas of service that require effort,

> Kids who are raised to make a wise choice about their mission in life are kids who learn to serve early.

sacrifice, and self-denial on an ongoing basis. Invariably, these children have made no such commitment.

Sadly, when I ask many of these parents where they themselves are serving, there's often nothing substantive either. There are always exceptions, but for the most part, kids who don't serve will grow up self-absorbed and hard to satisfy, and they will become quite unattractive and costly to the people around them. On the other hand, those with a true servant attitude exude *attractiveness and value* that make for endless possibilities of gaining success in the areas of fame, power, beauty, and wealth.

Bromide Prayers and Safe Trees

Embedded into the heart of an individual, these four anchor tenets of greatness—humility, gratefulness, generosity, and a servant attitude—give the grace within a person's heart the hands, feet, and voice it needs to change lives for God's glory. These take a vocation and turn it into a noble mission. These take our casual efforts on behalf of other people and turn them into running commentary on the love of God. We have the duration of our children's years under our roof to move these four anchor tenets from abstract concepts to the grit and fiber of their being.

And all we have to do is show them what they look like every day through our lives.

Should we drift off course, God occasionally brings along a friendly reminder of how true greatness behaves under pressure. I received just such a reminder in one of my weaker moments. It came at a corridor in my life when I was looking at my mission through the faulty filters of success.

He was about two-thirds my size, with black hair and dark bronze skin. His eyes were tucked back below a prominent forehead, and they sparkled in conjunction with his ear-to-ear grin. He was my prayer partner for the moment, but I was looking around to see if there might be someone more "conventional" to spend the next half hour with.

I was in Amsterdam. Darcy and I had been invited to gather with fifteen thousand evangelists and Bible teachers from all over the world to sharpen our skills and network our efforts.

There were passionate speakers who followed corporate worship to challenge us in our calling. Then there were breakout options that covered the gamut of needs that people who travel for the Lord's work tend to have. To double our efforts, Darcy and I decided to split up for the optional sessions and compare notes after we were back together. She was off to learn more about the administrative side of itinerant Christian work. I chose to learn about the power of prayer in ministry.

For about forty-five minutes, the presenter shared great insights from the Bible as well as his personal experiences on how to make prayer an ongoing force in our ministries. And then he shifted his lecture into a laboratory experience. He encouraged us to turn to the person next to us, exchange prayer needs, and then lift each other up before God. That's how I ended up with the diminutive young man from Sri Lanka with the permanent smile on his face. As I recall, he was very excited to be able to pray with me, an American. Shamefully, I have to confess that I wasn't as excited to pray with him.

It wasn't anything about him in particular that caused me to look to see if there might be another candidate to pray with. It's just that I . . . well, I didn't know why I didn't want to pray with him. I have to assume that deep down in my heart, I felt he had little to offer me. I was a prideful young preacher from America with more spending money in my pocket than this man saw in a year, and I didn't think we would relate to each other very well. As it turned out, I learned that I wasn't worthy to carry his Bible for him.

He slid over a couple of chairs to be right next to me, shook my hand, and introduced himself. His English had the heavy slur and accent distinctive to his region. He wanted to know all about me. When I told him about my wife and family, he asked if I had a picture. I did. He asked specific questions about each member of my family. And then he asked how he could pray for me. I gave him the normal safe stuff you give to strangers or people you don't want getting too close. "Pray that God will give me open doors and open hearts. Pray that God will watch over my family in my absence." He listened. He wrote down every word I said under my name on the inside flap of his Bible.

And then he prayed. Oh my, did he pray! He lifted me up with the strength and tenderness of a person who was clearly on a first-name basis with God. And then he wept as he asked God to watch over my family in my absence. He mentioned Darcy and each child by name. I found myself staring at him with my eyes wide open in amazement over his sincerity and passion. And then he whispered, "Amen."

I shifted myself uncomfortably in my seat, pulled out a small piece of scrap paper to write down what he said, and then asked him the same question he asked me earlier: "How can I pray for you?"

He was quiet for a moment. And then without fanfare or panache, he said, "Oh, Brother Tim! Please pray that when I come into a village to bring the precious good news of Christ's love and grace, I can find a *safe* tree to sleep in at night."

I was writing as he spoke. I started to write "safe . . ." and then stopped to look at him. "Safe tree? What's a safe tree?"

He said, "Oh, Brother Tim! One night I was deep asleep in a tree when I was suddenly awakened by a vicious reptile that had wrapped himself around me."

"What? What are you talking about?" He went on to explain how he had climbed into a tree to spend the night, and while he was asleep, a python had slipped into the tree and decided to have him for dinner. Pythons wrap themselves around their prey, suffocate them with their tremendous strength, and then consume them once their victim has stopped breathing. This young evangelist had put up the fight of his life and was able to escape. But he said since that night, he's had a difficult time drifting comfortably off to sleep in trees.

I asked the obvious questions that naive Americans ask: "Why don't you stay in a hotel?" Answer: They don't have such places in most of the villages he visits. Besides, if they did, they would require money that he seldom had to spare. "Why can't you stay in someone's home?" Answer: Most of the time, he is ministering in areas where Christianity is not welcomed. People could be persecuted by fellow villagers for inviting him in.

And so I prayed for this young man . . . for his ministry . . . and for him to get a safe night's sleep without fear of snakes. And then we parted into a sea of Christian workers, and I never saw him again. But he has never been far away from me since.

I've slept in hundreds of hotels in my career. I've never once drifted off to sleep wondering whether a snake might wrap itself around me during the night. There were times before I crossed paths with this evangelist from Sri Lanka that I actually found myself disappointed with room service at my hotel or with the fact that room service was closed by the time I checked in. There were times when the pillows weren't comfortable or the people in the halls were too noisy. There were even times when I took these frustrations to the Lord. But I can't say I was praying when I did it. I thought I was at the time, but I knew I wasn't after I met the young evangelist from Sri Lanka. Actually, what I was doing was whining. It happens more often than many of us think. Instead of focusing on the opportunities we have to be the light of the world and the salt of the earth in our careers, we focus on our inconveniences and pout about them.

There's no place for that kind of "praying" in the heart of a person whose mind is thoroughly fixed on Christ. I've grown a lot since that time. And I'm grateful to a little man from Sri Lanka for the inches that have been added to my spiritual height. He was a man who had found his "sweet spot." In the process, he helped me see what the attitude of a person who has chosen the right mission in life truly looks like.

There are some great guide wires that hold humility, grate-fulness, generosity, and a servant attitude firmly in place. My friend from Sri Lanka had them. Join me in the next chapter to find out what they are.

Ten Ways to Teach Your Teenagers to Put God First

1. Let them see you serving God with a joyful and uncomplaining attitude.
2. Encourage them to serve God in substantive and regular ways that cause them to lean on Him for strength and courage.
3. Avoid solving all of their problems for them. Force them to turn to God to sort out relational conflicts and cultural dilemmas.
4. Avoid placing unrealistic expectations on the youth leaders at your church. Regardless of the strengths or weaknesses of the program, make sure your kids are a positive presence in the youth group.
5. Permit your teenagers to wrestle with the more perplexing problems of life, remaining calm while their faith is on trial.
6. Let them find you reading the Bible on a daily basis and acting on what you are learning.
7. Don't be afraid to design dilemmas that force your kids to trust in God and test their faith (what movies they watch, what clothing they choose, working part-time in a very secular environment, etc.). Be careful to use your personal veto sparingly and graciously.

8. Encourage them to think big when it comes to trusting God for a major need in someone else's life or their own (health, money, safety, etc.).

9. Encourage them to team with other teenagers who believe in a big God and serve side by side with them (mission trips, inner-city outreaches, care for the unfortunate, etc.).

10. Humbly share some of your own battles about who was going to be the master of your life, and walk your children through the process you went through to arrive at your decision.

chapter ten

HELPING YOUR CHILDREN SUSTAIN A GREAT MISSION IN LIFE

t's one thing to talk about a great mission in life. But the last time I checked, talk is cheap. Reality has a nasty habit of sucker punching us. We do the math in our hearts, and the cost of true greatness blinks its toll on our internal calculators. Like the evangelist from Sri Lanka in the previous chapter, the pythons in the trees make you wonder if your mission in life is worth it.

Quitting while you're ahead isn't just some worn-out cliché; it's the modus operandi of the rank and file. Most people give up at the mere rumor of trouble. But why resign yourself and your kids to such a conventional and predictable existence when God wants to empower them to live truly extraordinary lives? He's already offered them infinite power to maintain their mission. All they need to do is trust Him when all hell breaks loose.

There are a few character traits you can add to your humility, gratefulness, generosity, and servant attitude that will help them stay in the game when everything around suggests that this might be a good time to cash in their chips. God gives our children regular opportunities to develop these qualities through their childhoods; in the same way, He gives us constant opportunities to model them for our kids.

Five Qualities of a Great Mission

To conclude our discussion on this big question—"What is your mission in life going to be?"—let's look at five qualities that temper our humility, deepen our gratefulness, put backbone in our generosity, and humanize our servant spirit.

Others-Orientation

One of the logical extensions of serving God is maintaining a clear focus on the needs and interests of whoever's near us. It's biblical. The apostle Paul put it this way: "When you do things, do not let selfishness or pride be your guide. Instead, be humble and give more honor to others than to yourselves. Do not be interested only in your own life, but be interested in the lives of others" (Philippians 2:3–4 NCV).

> When we help our children develop humility, they will always have friends, gain favor, and have doors open for them.

This is more than just looking outward; it's the art of making people feel valuable and loved. Jesus did it everywhere He went. Whether it was the high and mighty or the social outcasts,

Jesus had eyes that were quick to notice them, hands that were ready to help them, and a heart that was glad to enfold them.

When we help our children develop humility, they will always have friends, gain favor, and have doors open for them. We can show them what this looks like in how we treat both the foreigner and the familiar, the stranger at the gas pumps and the teenager at the convenience-store checkout. When our kids figure out that everyone matters, that each person has a name and behind each face is a story, it is going to make them phenomenally *attractive and valuable* when they bring this quality into their careers.

Trustworthiness

Kids who live for the greater mission of glorifying God become adults you can depend on. But they are dependable not only when things are going right; they are even more so when things take a turn for the worse. *Trustworthiness* and *integrity* make great synonyms. The thing about people of integrity is that they maintain their values even when everything around them tells them to take the cheater's way out. Truly great people don't lie to cover mistakes. They don't renege on commitments. They don't withhold material fact in order to benefit their position. In Psalm 15, David said that a person of trust and integrity "swears to his own hurt and does not change" (v. 4 NKJV).

Trustworthy people make great spouses, parents, friends, team members, and employees. Even more, they make great leaders. They are exactly the kind of people to whom others want to hand the keys to the most prestigious offices. The marketplace stands or falls on its ability to find worthy people to entrust its greatest assets to. That's why it's possible for your child to struggle academically and still end up with his or her name on the most influential doors in the business community. Money, goods, and services require trustworthy people in order to sustain themselves. Do your children a favor: teach them that part of their great mission in life is to be trustworthy. It's amazing how *attractive and valuable* it will make them.

Tenacity

People with a great mission in life don't give up. Because what they do is merely another way of sharing God's love and influence, they maintain a flintlike commitment to finishing what they started. Tenacity is so much easier when you're doing everything for God's glory and honor. Whether they get paid for what they're doing, do it as a favor, or do it simply because it's the right thing to do, tenacious people don't leave their post when the bullets start to fly.

Pastor Joel Osteen tells of a man whose mission in life was to work for God's glory, to use his gifts and skills for His honor, and to stay tenaciously focused on his assignment regardless of whether he got treated properly or gained the recognition he deserved. This man worked as a mechanic in a garage that exclusively serviced large eighteen-wheeled diesel trucks. Unfortunately, his work environment was negative, bawdy, and filled with ridicule; on top of that, he was mocked for the convictions that ruled his daily life. He was treated unkindly by his supervisor, and despite being the top producer for the company year after year, he went for seven years without receiving a pay raise or a bonus.

Did he get bitter? Did he nurse a grudge? Did he sue them

for unfair treatment in the workplace? He could have. Most people would have. He didn't. He had a higher calling. He was on a mission to serve the Lord Jesus. So he simply continued to do the best work possible, bite his lip, and trust himself to God, the righteous Judge. That's who he was primarily working for in the first place.

Then, out of the blue, his phone rang. It was the owner of the company. Because the owner had no participation in local operations, the two had never met personally. But that didn't mean the owner wasn't aware of the phenomenal asset this mechanic was to the company. After the owner introduced himself, he told the mechanic that he had decided to retire and was looking for the right person to take over the business. He told this mechanic that he wanted him to have it. Let's pick up the narrative from there:

"You know, sir, I'd love to have it," said the mechanic, "but I don't have enough money to buy your business."

"No, you don't under-stand," replied the owner. "You don't need the money. I have money. I'm looking for someone I can trust to continue the work I have started. I want to *give* it to you."

> Character glows in the dark. It's hard not to notice it.

Today, the mechanic owns that company free and clear! He says, "To this day I don't know how he got my name. I don't know why he chose me. All I know is that almost overnight, I went from being the lowest man on the totem pole to the person in charge of the whole company!"[1]

This mechanic didn't know why the owner chose him, but I

do. His greater mission in life made him a standout over the other mechanics and supervisors who were living and working for what they could get out of it. Integrity generates its own light. Character glows in the dark. It's hard not to notice it.

God does that all the time for people who are willing to serve Him and live for Him. Bible characters like Abraham, Joseph, Moses, Ruth, David, Esther, Daniel, and Paul come to mind. This mechanic was just one of a long line of people whose mission in life was to glorify God and shine for Him continually. He couldn't help but end up *attractive and valuable* to the powers that be.

Courage

My favorite definition of *courage* is the one attributed to John Wayne: "Courage is when you're scared to death, but you saddle up anyway." If you are going to help your kids live a mission that is bigger than life itself, you'd better build courage into their hearts.

This is hard to do if you are preoccupied with raising safe kids. As I've stated before, the job of parents is not to raise safe kids but to raise strong ones. Helping them learn to calculate risk and step out in faith should be center stage in your parenting curriculum.

Obviously, I'm not suggesting that you raise your kids in a reckless manner. There are clear and present dangers that we must protect them from and ultimately prepare them for. But you can't live a mighty mission for God if you aren't willing to entrust your circumstances as well as your fears to His safekeeping. If He is truly your master, you shouldn't be surprised that He asks you to do things that take the moisture out of your mouth and put a knot in your gut.

The summer before her senior year of high school, our daughter Shiloh worked in the inner city of Phoenix. Among other things, she helped a ministry that works at street level in some of the worst parts of that town. They were putting on weeklong day camps for children of various ages. One week was exclusively for the kindergarten and younger elementary school kids.

I need to qualify this story with a little inside information. Shiloh's life verse is Psalm 73:25–26: "Whom have I in heaven but you? And earth has nothing I desire besides you. My flesh and my heart may fail, but God is the strength of my heart and my portion forever." These verses define so much of Shiloh's mission in life.

In the first few weeks, she and several other interns canvassed the various neighborhoods to find kids who could come to day camp. In the process, she met a little boy (about five years old) who lived with eight adults in a trailer. She told the boy's mother about the day camp and made arrangements to pick him up on Monday of that week. She had drawn a picture of a giraffe and put it in one of the windows of her Jeep. In her limited Spanish, she said to the boy, "I'll be here on Monday morning to pick you up in my Giraffe mobile."

The morning came, the boy was ready, and the day was spent. He was quiet, shy, and guarded, but he had a nice time with Shiloh. She took him and several of the other children to Burger King for a treat. When she asked if he'd like some food with his ice cream, he nodded yes. He pointed to one of the huge adult meals on the menu. She watched this tiny boy devour the entire meal. Because of this and other factors that I can't elaborate on, there was every indication that this boy was not only lacking in basic nutrition but most likely enduring some frightening and abusive circumstances in his home. She took the boy home at the end of the day and told him that she'd be back to get him in the morning.

The next morning she rapped on the door, but no one responded. She rapped some more. Still no response. As she related this incident to her mother and me a week later, she said, "I'm not an invasive person. I have respect for people's space. And I don't like confrontation. But I had to do everything I could to get their attention. More importantly, I had to do everything I could to let that boy know that I had indeed come back to get him." Still no one came to the door.

"So you know what I did?"

"No. What?" we both responded.

"I did the cop knock!" she told us.

"The cop knock? What's that?" I asked.

Shiloh said, "That's where you make a fist and pound away on the doors, siding, and windows to get their attention."

"And did they answer the door?" we asked.

That's when she told us the rest of the story. She managed to get the mother once, an older sister another time, and one of the men another time. But they would not let the boy show his face and refused to let him go to camp. Most likely, they figured out that the boy might comment about abuses within his home to people who could actually do something about it. But something inside of Shiloh told her she had to go back for that boy each morning and do her best to get their attention to see if they'd let him come to camp. Every morning through the last day of that week of camp, Shiloh went back for that boy and did the "cop knock" to get their attention to see if they'd let him come.

She admitted that she was scared. She didn't want to do it, but she knew that for the little boy's sake, she had to make sure he knew that she didn't turn her back on him.

We, of course, voiced our concern for her safety and wondered about the wisdom of her taking those kinds of risks in such a dangerous neighborhood. That's when she reminded us that the ministry she works for teaches them what risks are appropriate and which ones aren't.

She went on to say, "Mom, Dad, it's the inner city. It's a hostile place. If you're going to let it intimidate you, you might as well go back to your safe, upper-middle-class, comfortable, Starbucks Christian community."

More important, she felt certain that in this situation, her mission for the Lord was to do everything to communicate to that little boy that there were some followers of God who loved him and were willing to take huge risks on his behalf.

I continued, however, to voice my concerns. "Shiloh, that was very dangerous."

"I know, Dad. And I would have much preferred to run away and not come back, because it was very frightening. But there was no doubt in my heart that God wanted me to return each morning. I felt I was doing what I was told."

"But, honey, the *risks*," I reminded her.

Then she silenced our concerns with these words: "Whom have I in heaven but you? And earth has nothing I desire besides you. My flesh and my heart may fail, but God is the strength of my heart and my portion forever."

Shiloh has all the credentials that most parents bank on to ensure their child a great future. She has fabulous grades and a full ride to a top-level university, she's a stellar athlete, she's been an elected leader of her peers throughout her school career, and she's beautiful. But these aren't why I am confident she will become a great adult. She'll be great because she serves a great master, and she's not hesitant to carry out His mission for her life. She's already far more *attractive and valuable* than we had ever hoped she'd be.

Compassion

People with a mission that is bigger than life have a sensitive heart toward the disconnected, disenfranchised, dejected, and discouraged. Whether it's a friend, a stranger, or even a detractor, people who live their lives for God care about others in need. Great people want to lighten people's burdens and dispense hope to everyone they can. From simple encouragement to harder things that actually cost them something, people who glorify God go out of their way to make life better for the people God puts in their path. For our kids, it means being a friend to the friendless, a shield to the defenseless, truth to the misinformed, arms and legs for the weak, and optimism to the hopeless.

Guess what? Kids who grow up into compassionate adults become *attractive and valuable* to all the key sectors of their grown-up world. They are also extremely contagious. Compassionate people not only raise people's spirits; they strengthen the desire of many people watching them to follow suit.

Turning Boys into Men

All of this talk of greatness and mission reminds me of someone. I met him a decade ago, shortly after he'd hung up his cleats and shoulder pads for good. His name is Joe Ehrmann. He had played defensive tackle for the Baltimore Colts and the Detroit Lions before retiring from professional football back in 1982. At the height of his career, Joe had a watershed experience that forced him to evaluate everything he held near and dear to him: his baby brother contracted cancer. When all the king's horses and all the king's men couldn't put his brother back together again, Joe found himself asking questions in the aftermath of his brother's passing that only God could answer. As a result, he gave his heart and everything attached to it to Jesus Christ. In the process, he developed an unusual philosophy about how to live life large.

For one thing, he saw the success fantasy for what it was—all promise and prize, but no purpose. Surrounded by the gods of the gridiron and the glitz of the gentrified who hover around the NFL, Joe stared into the eyes of fame, power, beauty, and wealth on a regular basis. He saw these things for the shell game that they are: nice things to be gained by default, but nothing worth aiming your life at. So you have money? So what? It just buys more stuff. So you crack heads on Sunday afternoon with the best of them? Big deal. Eventually, you'll have to retire to nurse your arthritis. So you seldom have to pay for your meal or pick up your bar tab in Baltimore? Whoopee. These things neither impressed Joe nor enticed him. That's because something eternal happened to him on a cross outside of Jerusalem, and he was convinced that his brief time on earth could be lived for something greater than the empty rewards of success.

That's what prompted Joe and his wife, Paula, to plant their family at street level on Baltimore's nasty east side. They could have easily holed up in some posh suburban mansion. But that would have required Joe to turn his back on a huge mission that God had laid on his heart. Joe saw the kids of the streets—in particular, the boys of the streets—like sheep without a shepherd. Racism, violence, and despair hovered over the projects. Young men moved in gangs, and young girls found themselves at their mercy. Hopelessness and helplessness became constants in most of these kids' lives.

Edmund Burke once said, "The only thing necessary for the triumph of evil is for good men to do nothing." Joe couldn't live with that option. He and his wife took up residence in this depressed section of Baltimore and turned on the lights. Brightly.

He founded "The Door," a nondenominational ministry that provides after-school and summer athletic, reading, tutoring, mentoring, substance abuse prevention, and family counseling programs. Two other projects were born from his passions: a Ronald McDonald House for families to live in while their sick children endure long stays in the hospital and a racial reconciliation project called Mission Baltimore. He also runs a foundation called Building Men for Others. It's a way of turning boys into men without the excess baggage of the success illusion.

Joe sees our young boys framed inside a flawed set of standards. In an interview in *Parade* magazine, Joe commented about the usual yardsticks of our culture—athletic ability, sexual conquest, and economic success:

> Those are the three lies that make up what I call "false masculinity." The problem is that it sets men up for tremendous failures in our lives. Because it gives us this concept that what

we need to do as men is compare what we have and compete with others for what they have.

Masculinity, first and foremost, ought to be defined in terms of relationships. It ought to be taught in terms of the capacity to love and to be loved. It comes down to this: What kind of a father are you? What kind of a husband are you? What kind of coach or teammate are you? What kind of a son are you? What kind of a friend are you? Success comes in terms of relationships.

And then all of us ought to have some kind of cause, some kind of purpose in our lives that's bigger than our own individual hopes, dreams, wants and desires. At the end of our life, we ought to be able to look back over it from our deathbed and know that somehow the world is a better place because we lived, we loved, we were other-centered, other-focused.[2]

Joe found the perfect context to transfer these characteristics of the truly great. Football. The game was second nature to him. But the concept of teaching love through football was not second nature to the game.

It is now.

Joe came alongside his best friend, Biff Poggi, the head coach of the Gillman Greyhounds, and started showing these kids from the projects how to love one another in the midst of one of the roughest games in high school. Joe volunteers as the defensive coach, but his bigger goal is to build these young athletes into great men. They use the context of football to teach the higher calling of community, relationships, and service to others.

Joe imprints on the hearts of these street-level athletes that "they will make the greatest impact on the world—will bring the most love and grace and healing to people—by constantly basing their actions and thoughts on one simple question: What can I do for you?"[3]

Just before the young men race out onto the field for the opening kickoff, you hear a strange back-and-forth between Coach Erhmann and his players.

"What is our job as coaches?"

"To love us!" the team yells in cadence.

"What is your job?" Joe asks.

"To love each other."

If you were to pull one of his defensive players aside and asked him what his job is on the field, he'd say, "Penetrate, pursue, punish, and love."

Sounds to me like Joe Erhmann has either lost his mind or cornered the essence of truly great coaching. The success illusion focuses on wins and losses, statistics, and championships. These don't find their way into the spotlight of the philosophy of coaching that has served Joe Ehrmann for over two decades.

When coaches and parents approach Joe about the bottom line of football—winning—he says, "Well, we've had pretty good success, but winning is only a by-product of everything else we do—and it's certainly not the way we evaluate ourselves."[4]

You'd have to pull the "bottom line" out of Joe, but, for the record, the Gilman Greyhounds went undefeated three out of six of the seasons under Joe's influence. For years they have been ranked number one in Maryland and have held a position in the top twenty high school teams in America in the national rankings for that same amount of time.

That's nice, but that's not the main reason Joe Erhmann does what he does. He has a passionate love for God that shows itself in an unquenchable love and concern for others. He's turning the grace in his heart into humility, gratefulness, generosity, and a servant's spirit that is making an eternal difference in young lives.

I don't know what your circumstances are—whether you are educated, sophisticated, well off, or well known. But since you're reading this book, I'd guess that you have someone for whom you are spending your time working through these words—a son or daughter, grandchild, or friend. Let me ask you something: What are these children living their lives for? What are you aiming them at? Regardless of who they are or what they do, if your children commit to living for God and for others, they will be assured a place in God's Hall of Greatness.

> Regardless of who they are or what they do, if your children commit to living for God and for others, they will be assured a place in God's Hall of Fame.

All you have to do is move your aim from the cultural target of success and focus your child on the much higher and nobler target of true greatness.

Some Closing Thoughts

True greatness. It's not about us. And it's certainly not about our kids. When we can get them to see this vital truth, we set them up to more likely choose a mission in life that enables them to make a huge difference and enjoy a great future.

This entire chapter can be distilled down to one word: *love*. When our mission in life is to love God and others, we can't go wrong. English philosopher Jeremy Bentham put it this way: "The way to be comfortable is to make others comfortable, the way to make others comfortable is to appear to love them, the way to appear to love them is to love them in reality."

But how do we do this? It's no secret. And though there are no guarantees that our children will make the right choice, we'll clearly make the possibility more likely for our children if we do the following.

Set an Example

Go back through chapters 9 and 10 and review the list of assets of people with a mighty mission in life. Then ask yourself, "How am I doing at modeling these qualities to my kids?" Honestly ask God to show you areas of your life where you demonstrate arrogance, a "me first" attitude, a lack of trust, ungratefulness, a tendency to easily give up, cowardliness, coldheartedness, stinginess, or an unwillingness to pull your fair share and serve other people's needs.

Ask God for forgiveness. Invite a few friends to be your mentors to improve your track record. Study the Bible in these areas. Ask God for His unlimited strength. Become a person of excellence, a person who goes the extra mile to do what's right. And finally, acknowledge your bad example to your kids. They know about it anyway. But when they can see a parent who is willing to make things right with God and with them, they are more likely to be willing to look honestly at themselves.

Encourage Your Children

The second thing you can do is to encourage your children to bring these qualities to the forefront of everything they do, be it

team sports, chores, home-
work, play, or interaction
with friends, strangers,
teachers, siblings, or you.
They're never too young to
begin learning how to live
for greatness. Even if they
are already well along in
their journey through

> Encourage your children
> to develop a passionate
> love for God that
> demonstrates itself in
> an unquenchable love
> and concern for others.

childhood, it's not too late to introduce these values to them.

Helping them develop these values is easier once they've
made the most important decision in their lives—to make God
their ultimate master.

Encourage your children to develop a passionate love for
God that demonstrates itself in an unquenchable love and concern for others. If you help them make this their mission in life,
I'll let you in on a little secret: your children are going to grow
up to be truly great adults.

Ten Ways to Be a Great Church Member (For Your Kids)

1. Make a decision in your heart to love going to church. That's all it takes. A decision. Once it's made, you'll love going to church.
2. Bring your Bible with you, and learn how to follow your teacher, pastor, or youth leaders as they teach you from it.
3. When you get up on Sunday morning, ask God to help you learn everything He wants you to learn at church that day.
4. Pray for your pastor, youth leaders, worship leaders, and Sunday school teachers at least once during the week. Ask God to bless them and encourage them in their efforts on behalf of the church.
5. Look out for the new kids, awkward kids, lonely kids, or outcast kids. Enfold them every time you are at a church gathering (whether formal or social).
6. If there is a discussion in class, participate in it. Don't just sit back and be unresponsive.
7. Always love, encourage, and cooperate with the people who work with you at church (whether professional or volunteer). Voice appreciation for their efforts. Always thank

your teacher for the lesson and the worship leaders for their efforts.

8. Refuse to speak disparagingly about anyone who works with or for you at church. Never participate in a critical discussion about them with friends or a friend's parents. If you have a problem with a leader, first take it to God in prayer and then go to the person individually and discuss it. Always rise above gossip.

9. Go to church with an attitude of what you can give to it rather than what you can get out of it. Go ready to help, to serve, to sing, to listen, to learn, to make new friends, to reach out to visitors, and to enjoy being with God's people.

10. Make sure that you always use your time at church to connect more closely to the heart of God.

THE TASTE OF TRUE GREATNESS

It's really quite simple. Our kids are going to end up *some-where*. And we are going to aim them at *something*. Why not *greatness*?

When you think of the alternatives, none seems worthy of kids brought up in the shadow of the cross. We all want our kids to grow up to embody a passionate love for God that shows itself in an unquenchable love and concern for others.

When it comes down to the honest feelings within our hearts, there's no debate—just one question.

Can I do it?

Can I, the person whose love for my children is second only to the God who created them and bought them on a cross, make the grade?

What's the matter? Are you thinking about those feet of clay you put your shoes over today? Don't worry about that; God has been using the weak to confound the wise since the beginning of time.

What about those regrets? You've got them stuffed in bags and suitcases that clutter the hallways and back rooms of your heart. How about once and for all lugging them to the foot of the cross, dumping them out, and letting Jesus dispose of them for good?

"But I'm still weighed down with inadequacies," you may protest. "My knowledge is limited, my experiences are flawed, and I can't seem to get a grip on those fears that lurk in the corners of my conscience."

I'd like to say, "Get in line . . . behind *me* and everyone else," but that doesn't address your legitimate concerns. All I know is that God has been drawing straight lines with crooked sticks ever since the thief who hung next to Him on the cross said, "Remember me when you come into your kingdom" (Luke 23:42).

> All you have to do to give your children this five-sense version of greatness is remember one thing:
>
> *Grace.*

Besides, raising kids for greatness is far less about what you do and far more about who you are. Moms and dads who decide to embody greatness are all a child really requires. Our kids just need an idea of what greatness looks like, feels like, tastes like, smells like, and sounds like.

And all you have to do to give your children this five-sense version of greatness is remember one thing:

Grace.

That's all this message is about. It's about taking the grace that God has given you and letting it permeate the pores of your life. Let it seep through your intellect, volition, emotions, and spirit. Let its humility, gratefulness, generosity, and servant attitude be the posture of your body, the position of your arms, and the constant expression on your face. When your kids experience God's grace through you on a daily basis, then grooming them for greatness will be easy.

God did a great forgiveness for you. He did a great transformation in you. And He wants to do a great work through you. Let Him do it. Give Him your attitude, and let Him squeeze out all the self, confusion, second-guessing, and fear . . . just let Him wring it out of you. In its place, let the attitude of a *great* parent shine in everything you do.

Love big!
Work hard!
Forgive gladly!
Repent quickly!
Encourage graciously!
Speak humbly!
Play enthusiastically!
Think abundantly!
And . . . never stop dancing!

Your willingness to lead the way to greatness will give your children the best chance possible to follow in your footsteps. They'll grow up to make good choices about their missions, their mates, and their master. And someday, you'll slip the surly bonds of this life to take your rest in the company of the God for whom you did all of this.

Don't be surprised if He's waiting for you when you arrive. He'll be the one who can't wait to wrap His gentle arms around you, pat your weary head with His nail-scarred hands, and whisper in your ear, "Way to go, good and faithful friend.

You took the life that I gave you and the children I left in your care, and you handed them all back to Me to do with as I thought best. Thanks for trusting Me. You turned My grace into a greatness that made their lives eternally significant. I've been looking forward to your arrival and this opportunity to personally thank you for a job well done. Welcome home!"

Ten Ways to Help Your Kids Get the Best Out of Organized Sports

1. Avoid keeping statistics on your kids' performance. That's what parents who are wrapped up in the success fantasy do. Just keep encouraging your child to play hard, fair, and passionately and to be a good member of the team.
2. Always encourage your children to respect and obey the coach, regardless of the coach's effectiveness.
3. Never upbraid umpires or referees regarding a call they've made. They're humans. If you think a bad call has been made, accept it and move on. Remember, it's just a game.
4. Avoid getting involved in any disparaging discussions with other parents about coaches, athletes, officials, umpires, or other parents. Encourage them to support these people instead of talking negatively about them.
5. Make your children finish their commitment to a season, even if they aren't enjoying themselves. This will be great practice for their future lives when they'll be called on to finish a lot of commitments that aren't any fun.

6. Encourage all of the kids on the team, not just your child.

7. Be sensitive to the kids who may not have a lot of support from their parents or are having stress in their family. Give them rides to and from practices and games. Invite them (and their parents) to join you after games for ice cream.

8. If your kids are on a winning team, remind them that humility should be their ongoing attitude. Discourage your children from gloating in victory or basking in applause.

9. Don't allow your children to show off when they've performed well. They're supposed to do their best. Teach them to win with graciousness.

10. If your children are on a losing team, don't criticize the coach. Instead, encourage the coach and say how much you appreciate the effort he or she is putting into your child and the team as a whole.

Bonus: Don't focus your children on winning. Focus them on playing their best and working in harmony with the team, and the victories will take care of themselves. Greatness beats success every time.

Study Guide:
Let's Talk About Greatness!

This book may have been written with the individual in mind, but it's a blast to study as a group. The subject of greatness is one of those bigger-than-life desires that all parents should have for their children. When you pool your thoughts and ideas with others, there is no limiting the many ways this concept of true greatness can teach you, grow you, and empower you to make it one of the center-stage commitments of your life.

To make your discussions more effective, I've divided the questions for each chapter into three parts:

- **Get the Discussion Going**—questions that break the ice on the chapter everyone just read;
- **Taking It Deeper**—questions designed to interact directly with points and principles developed in the chapter;
- **Making Greatness a Way of Life**—questions that help you turn what you've read into specific actions you can apply immediately.

The only thing I suggest is that you don't let the questions hold you hostage. Don't feel you have to do them all, and don't feel that you're confined to only these questions. If you have questions of your own that you want to discuss as a group, go for it! And if you feel you didn't get enough time to discuss the chapter as thoroughly as you wanted, don't be afraid to revisit it the next time you get together. Set a pace that enables you to get all that this message has to offer.

Are you ready? Let's talk about greatness!

Why Success Isn't Enough

Getting the Discussion Going

1. Most people have high admiration for people like Mother Teresa, yet few people would want to trade places with her for more than a couple of hours. What does that say about our deeper spiritual beliefs?

Taking It Deeper

1. If it is true that most parents don't lead their children to high standards of service toward others, what are some of the negative trade-offs when it comes to their children's attitude toward God? Their view of themselves? Their attitude toward their parents' leadership?

2. In what ways do churches today promote the culture's priorities of success?

3. In the chart that contrasts success with true greatness, why do you think many parents gravitate toward the "success" side of the chart even though the "true greatness" side looks far nobler?

Making Greatness a Way of Life

1. What is one principle you learned from this chapter that can help you build a sense of true greatness into your children?

chapter one

THE LONG AND WINDING ROAD TO GREATNESS

Getting the Discussion Going

1. What are the philosophies within our culture that make it so difficult to maintain an attitude of service toward others? Within our churches? Within our hearts?

2. How did Jesus describe true greatness in Matthew 20:25–28? In what ways is Jesus's definition of *greatness* different than the world's definition?

Taking It Deeper

1. What are some things that parents do that unwittingly push children toward an attitude of wanting to be served by others rather than wanting to serve others?

2. How much of what we do as parents teaches our children to work for a heavenly reward as opposed to an earthly one?

3. Of the three big questions facing our children (mission, mate, master), which one do you find the most difficult to equip your child to answer? Why?

Making Greatness a Way of Life

1. If an outsider were objectively evaluating your calendar, checkbook, attitude, heart, and reputation, would he conclude that you are aiming your kids at success or at true greatness? How would he build his case?

2. Why do you think it is so easy for people of faith to get drawn into our culture's love affair with the standard goals of success (wealth, beauty, power, and fame)?

chapter two

FINE-TUNING OUR IDEA OF GREATNESS

Getting the Discussion Going

1. What are some of the lessons that the heroes of 9/11 taught us when it comes to the stark differences between success and true greatness?

2. If life is an unending struggle for meaning, purpose, and hope, why do the normal targets of success fall short when it comes to satisfying these deep longings?

Taking It Deeper

1. In the days of Moses, John the Baptist, and Jesus, many parents within the nation of Israel were aiming their children at the standard features of success. How do success-oriented parents undermine God's greater purposes of God in the church today?

2. Tim referred to vulnerable moments in our children's lives— when they're asleep, being dumped by a boyfriend/girlfriend, injured, or sick. What do these moments tell you about your deepest longings for your child?

3. Moses is a great reminder that it may take many years of deliberate work before you see any real payoff for your efforts of raising kids for true greatness. Success, on the other hand, often gives easy and immediate positive results. What are the internal battles you fight when it comes to leaning your efforts one way or the other?

Making Greatness a Way of Life

1. Of the "Ten Ways to Be a Great Employee," which one do you find most difficult to carry out? Why?
2. What is one principle you learned from this chapter that can help you build a sense of true greatness into your children?

chapter three

THE SUCCESS ILLUSION

Getting the Discussion Going

1. What are some of the negative by-products of falsely equating wealth with greatness when it comes to our role as parents?

2. What are some of the ways the Christian environment has unwittingly accommodated our appetite for the "success illusion"?

Taking It Deeper

1. The piety of the Pharisees led them into the trap of self-righteousness. This is often the by-product of how we measure a person's commitment to God. What are some of the superficial standards that we embrace in our Christian circles that cause us to fall short of genuine spiritual greatness? Read Mark 12:38–40 and Luke 18:9–14 to gain some insight.

2. What do you think Jesus was trying to say in Luke 17:33 regarding the folly of pursuing fame?

3. How much does the priority of looks and beauty play into your attitude toward your children? How do you think that affects their spiritual beliefs? Their attitude toward you?

Making Greatness a Way of Life

1. What are some of the priorities of your parenting efforts that may end up in eternity's Dumpster?

2. What are some specific things you can do to offset the constant barrage your children receive from their culture regarding the trophies of success?

chapter four

THE PARADOX OF TRUE GREATNESS

Getting the Discussion Going

1. What are some specific ways that God's economy runs counter to our culture's? How does this complicate your role as a parent trying to raise kids for true greatness? (See Isaiah 55:8.)

2. How does focusing our children on the priorities of success push our kids toward an attitude of arrogance? How do you think it affects the impact of their faith?

Taking It Deeper

1. Tim says, "Our attitude toward doing the work of God's ministry in our church should be to do whatever we can, forget who gets credit for it, and pray that God gets all the glory." What do you find is your biggest obstacle to living out this kind of attitude in front of your kids?

2. Tim talked about making "grace" our native tongue. What role do you think grace plays in raising kids for true greatness? In what specific ways can you model grace to your children?

3. Like the desperate boy with the brick, God sometimes takes drastic steps to show us the folly of our thinking. Has God ever used extreme measures to get your attention? What was He trying to show you? How well did it work?

Making Greatness a Way of Life

1. What is the biggest insight you gained from this chapter when it comes to the priorities you are embracing as a parent?

2. Of the "Ten Ways to Be a Great Teammate," which one do you find most difficult to instill into your child? Why?

chapter five

RELEASE THE SECRET WEAPON

Getting the Discussion Going

1. How does the pursuit of success handicap our children's ability to be the kind of friends God has truly called them to be?

2. What is it about the characteristics of true greatness (humility, gratefulness, generosity, servant attitude) that makes a person so attractive to others? What are some of the ways our culture coaches us away from building these traits into our children?

Taking It Deeper

1. Read the scriptures listed for *humility* (1 Peter 5:5–6; Micah 6:8; Proverbs 15:33) and *gratefulness* (James 1:17–18; Philippians 4:11–13), and then discuss other ways that humility can be carried out by our children besides the ones listed in this chapter.

2. Read the scriptures listed for *generosity* (Luke 6:38; 1 Corinthians 13:4–5; Colossians 3:12–14) and *servant attitude* (Philippians 2:3–4; John 13:4–5, 12–17; Matthew 25:37–40) and then discuss other ways that generosity and a servant attitude can be carried out by our children besides the ones listed in this chapter.

3. Tim says, "God has not called us to raise safe kids; He's called us to raise strong ones." How can the preoccupation with trying to protect our children from the culture undermine our ability to build true greatness into their character?

Making Greatness a Way of Life

1. Of the "Ten Ways to Be a Great Classmate," which one do you find most difficult to instill into your child? Why?
2. What is one principle you learned from this chapter that can help you build a sense of true greatness into your children?

chapter six

LIVING LARGE BY THINKING BIG

Getting the Discussion Going

1. Read John 6:1–14. What are some personal and practical things God teaches about true greatness through this passage?
2. Based on Tim's overview of abundant thinkers, do you think they are more or less born that way (it's their personality), or do you think this attitude can be cultivated regardless of a child's personality traits?

Taking It Deeper

1. Did scarcity thinking play any role in your family of origin? How did it affect your view toward yourself? Your siblings? Your future? God?
2. How does abundant thinking enhance your relationship with your children? Your spouse? Your relationship with God?
3. How much do you think fear plays into the mind-set behind scarcity thinking? What are the fears that block you from being the kind of abundant thinker you'd like to be for your children?

Making Greatness a Way of Life

1. What are some specific ways you could build an abundant mind-set into your children?
2. Of the "Ten Ways to Be a Great Friend," which one do you find most difficult to practice on a consistent basis? What is one thing you could do to overcome this problem?

chapter seven

HELPING YOUR CHILDREN CHOOSE A GREAT MASTER IN LIFE

Getting the Discussion Going

1. Why do you think so many people of faith are easily lured into the assumption that God wants to bless us with wealth and ease? How does this confuse our children's understanding of true greatness?

2. If life is not about us and is instead all about God, what are some specific ways we could teach this profound truth to our children on a daily basis?

Taking It Deeper

1. Tim says, "Every last one of us is in a state of servitude to someone or something." If it's true, what role do you think servanthood plays in our ability to model true greatness to our children? (You may want to reread Matthew 20:25–28.)

2. In what ways have you seen your bent toward selfishness block your ability to model true greatness to your children? What do you do to counter this natural tendency?

3. Tim listed some of the truly great people from the Bible: Abraham, Joseph, Ruth, David, Esther, and Daniel. If you're familiar with these Bible heroes, which one's life is closest to the life you have been called to live? What can you learn from that person when it comes to living out true greatness?

Making Greatness a Way of Life

1. In the list of common misunderstandings about God, has one or more of them affected your role as a parent? Which ones? What are some specific ways you could overcome a flawed or limited view of God?

chapter eight

HELPING YOUR CHILDREN CHOOSE
A GREAT MATE FOR LIFE

Getting the Discussion Going

1. In what ways do you think instilling the characteristics of true greatness into your children (humility, gratefulness, generosity, and a servant spirit) will enhance their ability to marry someone with similar commitments?

2. Tim says, "The key to finding the right mate is being the right kind of person." Do you really think it is that simple? How does who we are affect whom we attract?

Taking It Deeper

1. Do you find yourself torn between allowing God to lead your child to his or her ideal mate and wanting to try to steer the process? Why do we tend to feel like we need to manipulate this part of our children's lives? How is it working for you?

2. Do you find it easy or difficult to trust God to decide and direct the earning capacity of your married children?

3. What are some specific ways that we can walk our children through their battle with hormones rather than merely set a high standard and leave them to battle it alone?

Making Greatness a Way of Life

1. Tim says, "The best wedding gift we can give our children is to show them what a great married couple looks like." How are you doing on this? What are some specific things you can do to improve the example your children have? If you've been through a divorce, what are some specific ways you can minimize the negative effects of it?

chapter nine

HELPING YOUR CHILDREN CHOOSE
A GREAT MISSION IN LIFE

Getting the Discussion Going

1. Although Tim is all for children getting a good education, he believes that many parents overemphasize education at the expense of raising more well-rounded and therefore more valuable kids. How does our culture's worship of education undermine our ability to raise truly great kids? How can we counter these influences?

2. In what ways is developing a sense of mission into our children's lives more valuable than merely preparing them to make a great living when they grow up?

Taking It Deeper

1. What are the biggest factors keeping your children from hitting their "sweet spot" when it comes to their mission in life? What are some things you can do to counter these factors?

2. In what ways does raising kids to have an eternal mission in life enhance their ability to succeed at their temporal mission? (See John 10:10; Romans 5:2–4.)

Making Greatness a Way of Life

1. How are you doing at building an environment of fun, excitement, laughter, and grace into the context of helping your kids be academically prepared for the future? How do you think you could improve this?

chapter ten

HELPING YOUR CHILDREN SUSTAIN A GREAT MISSION IN LIFE

Getting the Discussion Going

1. Read Philippians 2:3–4. Does having this kind of "others orientation" come easy to most parents? What are some specific things parents can do to instill this powerful quality into their kids?

2. What is it about us that inclines us to err on the side of raising our kids in a safe environment—not necessarily a *strong* one—while they're living under our roof? What effect do you think "safe parenting" has in the long-term development of courage and true greatness in the hearts of our children?

Taking It Deeper

1. Psalm 15:4 says that trustworthy people "swear even to their own hurt and do not change." This includes the promises we made in our marriage, in legal contracts, with our employer or customers, and so on. How does our success-driven culture work against this truly great mind-set? What are some ways you can help your children live out this principle of trustworthiness?

2. What are the things in your background or your present circumstances that make it difficult for you to maintain a tenacious attitude toward the commitments God has given you?

3. If *courage* is as John Wayne said, "When you're scared to death, but you saddle up anyway," in what areas do you find yourself having to saddle up and ride into the middle of truly frightening situations? How do you see God using these to

build your children's commitment to true greatness? (You may want to reread Psalm 73:25–26.) If you cower from these callings, what do you think will be the price tag to your kids' view of true greatness?

Making Greatness a Way of Life

1. Tim suggests some specific things to do to turn around years of pursuing the success illusion: ask God for forgiveness, get mentors, ask God for His unlimited strength, become a person of excellence, and acknowledge your bad example to your kids. If this sounds like something you need to do, what are some specific ways you can put this plan into action?

2. Of the "Ten Ways to Be a Great Church Member," which one do you find most difficult to instill into your child? Yourself? Why?

The Taste of True Greatness

Getting the Discussion Going

1. Having read this book, what do you think about the idea of raising kids for true greatness?

Taking It Deeper

1. How has the concept of raising kids for true greatness changed the way you view yourself as a parent or grandparent?
2. What are the biggest obstacles keeping you from embracing a philosophy of parenting that emphasizes true greatness over success? What are you going to do about these obstacles?
3. How important is the exercise of day-to-day grace to the transferring of a truly great mind-set to your children?

Making Greatness a Way of Life

1. What is the most important thing God has shown you through the study of this book?
2. What are the most significant changes you will make in your role as a parent or grandparent now that you've read this book?
3. Based on what you've learned from this book, how are you going to be different as a person, outside your role as a parent or grandparent?

NOTES

Introduction: Why Success Isn't Enough

1. Ralph Wiley, "No One Faster Than Speeding Bullet," *ESPN Page 2*, http://espn.go.com/page2/s/wiley/020920.html. Accessed November 7, 2005.
2. Gabe Mirkin, M.D., "Bob Hayes' Flat Feet," http://www.drmirkin.com/fitness /1476.html. Accessed November 7, 2005.
3. Columbia University study, http://alcoholism.about.com/cs/tipsforparents/ a/blcasa030904_p.htm.

Chapter 3: The Success Illusion

1. For a deeper look at this subject, you might want to read my book *The High Cost of High Control* (Scottsdale, AZ.: Family Matters, 2005). You can find it at www.familymatters.net.

Chapter 5: Release the Secret Weapon

1. For a more detailed discussion on how to parent with grace, you might want to peek at the book I wrote on the subject, entitled *Grace-Based Parenting: Set Your Family Free* (Nashville: W Publishing Group, 2004).

Chapter 7: Helping Your Children Choose a Great Master in Life

1. Rick Warren, *The Purpose-Driven Life* (Grand Rapids: Zondervan, 2002), 1.

Chapter 8: Helping Your Children Choose a Great Mate for Life

1. Thomas J. Stanley, *The Millionaire Mind* (Kansas City: Andrews McMeel, 2001), 23.
2. H. Norman Wright and Wes Roberts, *Before You Say "I Do": A Marriage Preparation Manual for Couples* (Eugene, OR.: Harvest House, 1997).

Chapter 9: Helping Your Children Choose a Great Mission in Life

1. Marcus Buckingham, *The One Thing You Need to Know* (New York: Free Press, 2005), 202.
2. Ron Jensen, *Make a Life, Not Just a Living: 10 Timeless Skills to Help You Maximize Your Real Net Worth* (Nashville: Broadman and Holman, 2000).
3. Thomas J. Stanley, *The Millionaire Mind* (Kansas City: Andrews McMeel, 2001), 87.
4. One of the books that outlines these laws of money best is Ron Blue's book *Master Your Money: A Step-by-Step Plan for Gaining and Enjoying Financial Freedom* (Chicago: Moody, 2004).
5. Tim Kimmel, *Why Christian Kids Rebel: Trading Heartache for Hope* (Nashville: W Publishing Group, 2004).

Chapter 10: Helping Your Children Sustain a Great Mission in Life

1. Joel Osteen, *Your Best Life Now* (New York: Warner Faith, 2004), 166–67.
2. Jeffery Marx, "He Turns Boys into Men," *Parade*, August 29, 2004.
3. Ibid.
4. Ibid.

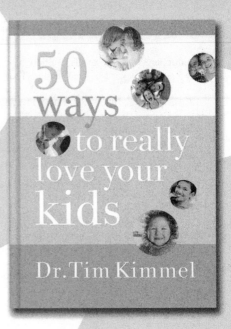

Parent your children the way
God parents His children:

with TENDERNESS, FORGIVENESS, AND GRACE.

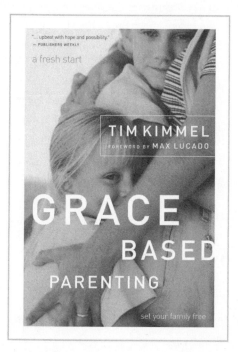

N ow Dr. Tim Kimmel, founder of Family Matters ministries, offers a refreshing new look at parenting. Rejecting rigid rules and checklists that don't work, Dr. Kimmel recommends a parenting style that mirrors God's love, reflects His forgiveness, and displaces fear as a motivator for behavior. As we embrace the grace God offers, we begin to give it—creating a solid foundation for growing morally strong and spiritually motivated children.

Now available in an affordable trade paper edition, this revolutionary book presents a whole new way to nurture a healthy family.

AVAILABLE WHEREVER BOOKS ARE SOLD.

W PUBLISHING GROUP
A Division of Thomas Nelson Publishers
Since 1798
www.wpublishinggroup.com

ABOUT THE AUTHOR

Dr. Tim Kimmel and his wife, Darcy, are the founders of Family Matters®. Committed to equipping families to appropriate the power of God's grace for every age and stage of life, Tim is one of America's top advocates speaking for the family today. He has sold more than 750,000 books and videos including the 2005 Gold Medallion winner *Grace Based Parenting, Why Christian Kids Rebel,* and his best-seller *Little House on the Freeway.* Tim has hosted his own nationally syndicated radio program, speaks to families across the country, and enjoys life with his wife, his four children, and his growing number of grandchildren.

ALSO AVAILABLE FROM TIM KIMMEL

Little House on the Freeway

Raising Kids Who Turn Out Right

Home Grown Heroes: Practical Principles for Raising Courageous Kids

The High Cost of High Control

Basic Training for a Few Good Men

Grace-Based Parenting

Why Christian Kids Rebel

Fifty Ways to Really Love Your Kids

Video Series

The Hurried Family

Raising Kids Who Turn Out Right

Basic Training for a Few Good Men

Grandparenthood: More Than Rocking Chairs

Tim can be reached through Family Matters:
www.familymatters.net